CONTENTS

Discover Chicago!

*The city has outlived its own legends:
the ganster-run metropolis has become a lively
commercial centre*

"**P**ork butchers for the world" wrote Carl Sandburg in his famous poem about Chicago, "tool makers, storers of corn, playing with railways and distributing the nation's freight, stormy, impolite and extremely noisy. A city where you need to have broad shoulders". We have each of us heard all these things about Chicago. Old pictures portray the city as murky, eerie and oppressive, and we think of John Dillinger and Al Capone and the rattle of tommy guns. The wind howls through the streets. "Windy City", the nickname sticks although not everybody likes it. In the height of summer the heat melts the asphalt pavements and in winter heaps of ice pile up on the banks of Lake Michigan. Shadowy pictures come to life. Thousands of cattle in the loading sheds outside the city. Endless goods trains. Bloody business in the abattoirs. The rattling of the elevated railway.

City of the blues, art and architecture: it is never boring in the "Windy City"

Gang wars, shootings and race riots. Just like Chicago, isn't that what you say when describing deplorable events occurring somewhere or other? What on earth are you doing in a city like that?

Of course, everything is quite different from that in Chicago. What a surprise it is when you come to the city for the first time and all your preconceptions are completely dispelled. It is true that the legendary slaughter houses did exist, but today they are but ruins. The cattle loading ramps are no more. John Dillinger and Al Capone are long since dead, and the crime rate in Chicago is less than that in many other cities. The race riots of the 1960s also belong to the past. There remain the extreme climate and the nerve-shattering rattle of the elevated railway which should have been demolished long ago. There are still the dirty quarters in the south and Madison Street with its drunks sleeping in house doorways. There remains the murky atmosphere of the suburbs where you go down dark iron steps into a blind labyrinth

5

of dark streets. Many visitors there are overcome by fear, although at the bottom of the steps they usually meet some quite nice people. Generally speaking, people make the best of things in Chicago and are more friendly than New Yorkers and have a better sense of humour. In the late 1960s a troupe of cabaret artists called themselves "The Second City", meaning Chicago was the second city after New York. But many Chicago-dwellers laugh up their sleeves at this and are quite convinced that they have long lived in city number one. They already have one of the tallest skyscrapers in the world. Chicago stretches for 30 miles along Lake Michigan and is home to some 2,800,000 people – covering an area equal to two thirds of New York City.

In the 17th century Louis Jolliet and Father Jacques Marquette were the first men to set foot on the banks of Lake Michigan, where Chicago was later to be built. At that time there were just a few Indian huts in the midst of wide expanses of grassland and forest in which grew masses of wild bulbs. Thus the Chippewas named the place "Shegahg", the "land of the wild bulbs". Later this Indian word became Chicago. Another school of thought says that a similar sounding Indian word meaning "powerful and strong" was in fact used to describe the power and influence of the local tribal chiefs. In 1673 Jacques Marquette built a mission here. The region remained under French rule until the late 18th century, then came American settlers and the army built a fort to protect the settlement from Indian uprisings. Fort Dearborn lay where the junction of Michigan Avenue and Wacker Drive now is. Once the base was attacked by Indians, and the war of 1812 also spelt danger for the American settlement. Gradually the Indians were driven out, the French and British withdrew and Chicago grew into a township of 40,000 inhabitants. On 4 March 1837 it was officially declared a municipality, and fifty years later it was the second largest in the USA.

As it grew in size so did its problems. Living conditions were bad, and there was a lot of poverty within its boundaries. This situation did not change until the building of the railway and the opening of the Ilinois & Michigan Canal. The city became the nation's largest cattle-loading station as well as a traffic junction and flourishing trade centre. More and more people streamed into Chicago searching for somewhere to live and a job. Nowhere else was as much money made as here, especially after the Civil War, when twice as much wheat was available as before and the dealers became more and more prosperous. Speculators made a lot of money. Factory owners and their well-dressed wives strolled through the parks, and everywhere the talk was solely about money. It seemed that nothing could stand in the city's way until in 1871 a catastrophe occurred which put even the San Francisco earthquake in the shade. In the Great Fire of Chicago more than 200 people

Downtown Chicago, the Loop, serves as an open-air gallery

lost their lives and over 90,000 lost their homes and all their possessions. The damage amounted to 200 million dollars.

The catastrophe left cruel traces in Chicago but was also to put the people of the city to the test. There was a total financial crash followed by a completely unexpected economic miracle which completely revitalised the city. Internationally renowned architects took advantage of the situation to plan the tallest and boldest of buildings for the new metropolis. As later in post-war Germany, the people rolled up their sleeves and and cleared away the debris. Within a few years they had built a new Chicago. The Water Tower, the only building to survive the conflagration unscathed, became a symbol of the undaunted determination of the city and its citizens.

So, after the fire, Chicago became an experimental field for creative and avant-garde architects and artists. Architects and master builders streamed in from all parts of the United States and even from Europe to help with the reconstruction. They were determined to make it one of the most attractive cities in the world. They had the advantage of not being restricted by official regulations as were their colleagues in many other towns. So nobody was surprised when back in 1885 William Le Baron Jenny erected a ten-storeyed building of steel and stone at the corner of La Salle and Monroe Street, which at the time was an almost revolutionary undertaking. The experiment was a success. The Home Insurance Building was more stable than all the others, and the concept of the skyscraper was born. Unfortunately the building fell victim to the rebuilding mania of later generations.

New trends were also set in motion by the World Columbia Exposition, a huge world exhibition held in 1893 which documented in an ideal manner the economic miracle which had helped Chicago to a new level of prosperity after the conflagration. In the first decade of the 20th century the population had already exceeded the two million mark and there was an almost unnerving upswing in trade. Electric trains ran on high rails, a giant railway station was opened and the film industry discovered the city. The cultural scene simply exploded and its theatrical productions and concerts could match the best in Europe. It was not until Black Friday in 1929 that the stock exchange crash heralded the end of the period of general afflu-ence – not just in Chicago but in the whole of America. During prohibition in the 1930s only organised crime made a constant profit. Gangster bosses like Al Capone and John Dillinger also made their home in Chicago. The prosperous economic centre became a gangster city which the film industry chose as the setting for its productions of the "Black Series". The city still suffers from this reputation even today. Who does not think of Edward G. Robinson and Humphrey Bogart when anyone mentions Chicago?

But Chicago is much more beautiful and better than its reputation suggests. The skyline with its slender skyscrapers has a certain fascination, especially when seen from the lake, and inside the Loop lies the centre of Chicago, a circle bordered by the lines of the elevated railway which stretches over 35 blocks, and in the north and west by the river, in the south by the elevated railway and in the east

Where stressed city-dwellers can relax: the banks of Lake Michigan

by Michigan Avenue. Within these natural limits lies the very hub of Chicago's business life. There stands the giant Sears Tower, until recently the world's tallest building, in which 16,000 people work, a city within a city. State Street boasts probably the longest pedestrian zone in the world, State Street Mall, seven blocks long, with department stores, shops, boutiques, record shops, bakeries, restaurants, cafés, cinemas and theatres. There are 32 sculptures by world-famous artists which simply stand on the pavements. For example one 16 m made for the people of Chicago by no less a person than Pablo Picasso and which has since become a city symbol, or "Flamingo", the giant red one by Alexander Calder in front of the Chicago Federal Center, or "The Four Seasons", a 20 m long mosaic by Marc Chagall at the First National Bank. As well as these, Henry Moore and Joan Miró – artists recognised worldwide – are represented in this open-air gallery.

The Loop is a busy island in the middle of the city, a noisy oasis in a noisy metropolis, a vital centre and a source of culture, commerce and communications. The rattling of the "El" (elevated railway), as we know it from the already mentioned crime films of the Black Series. The clatter of pneumatic drills at a building site in Adams Street. Queues of people at the bus stops. Streams of people on the metal staircases going up to the elevated railway. Folk are rushing and running everywhere. And in their midst others sit daydreaming on a bench or gaze interestedly at a sculpture by Calder. It is these contrasts that make the city so interesting, so alive.

The 1960s – an era of emergence in California – brought with them a certain degree of stagnation. Chicago had its problems.There was unrest in the black quarters and many people moved out to the suburbs. The only highlight of the early sixties was the building of the giant O'Hare International Airport, which inspired a new feeling of optimism, but it was the end of the decade before people moved back in numbers into the inner city. The John Hancock Center was built, with its hundreds of floors making it the fifth tallest building in the world. The gigantic Sears Tower was constructed by Skidmore, Owings & Merrill in the 1970s and for a long time was the world's tallest edifice. It is a particularly beautiful skyscraper, a slender dark tower of varying geometric forms, elegant and purpose-built and with a viewing platform on the top floor. Almost futuristic is the James R. Thompson Center by the Bavarian architect Helmut Jahn. This asymmetrical edifice of steel and glass on Lake Street towers up like a giant spaceship. Opinions are still divided regarding this visionary creation, but all recognise the courage and creativity of the Bavarian architect who was also responsible for the glass inner courtyard so flooded in light which forms part of the nearby Chicago Board of Trade building. "Life should be a great celebration of light and colour" said Helmut Jahn, while adding

"I was fortunate. The politicians were liberal and open-minded. Today it would no longer be possible to design such a building".

Outside the Loop the city can breathe more easily, it seems more liberal and open, especially on magnificent Michigan Avenue. On the one side tower the Loop skyscrapers, on the other the street leads to Grant Park and the apparently bankless Lake Michigan. The strong wind in no way diminishes the sparkle of of this boulevard because it seems to come to rest suspended between the houses leaving the northern part of the city unaffected. On the far side of the Chicago River expensive boutiques, luxury hotels and exclusive restaurants lie in wait for customers. Brown signs reading "Historic Route 66" mark Jackson Street and Adams Street and the route of the legendary street which was built in the 1820s and led from Chicago to Los Angeles. Cicero, a suburb of dilapidated houses and warehouses, still appears to resound with the echo of of the gunshots fired by Al Capone and Company on St Valentine's Day. And in your mind you can still hear the same music: sad blues tunes with accordions and subdued percussion, backed by a black voice the melancholy of which is never lost in the rattle of the elevated railway. The "blues" has made its home in Chicago, having left Memphis or New Orleans many years ago, and now forms part of the city more than any other music. Muddy Waters lived in Chicago and the world famous clarinettist Benny Goodman was born here. Blacks dominate in Chicago, and their music has become the city's soundtrack; on the little stage in B.L.U.E.S. on North Halsted, in the Checkerboard Lounge on South Side, where the music still has a genuine and unfalsified sound, and in the elegant Kingston Mines. Rock, folk and country do not really belong, although they are played quite a lot, especially in the dance clubs along North Lincoln Avenue. Apart from New York and New Orleans, there is no other US city where the "live scene" is so lively or where there are so many pubs and clubs.

In the spirit of Marco Polo

Marco Polo was the first true world traveller. He travelled with peaceful intentions forging links between the East and the West. His aim was to discover the world and explore different cultures and environments without changing or disrupting them. He is an excellent role model for the travellers of today and the future. Wherever we travel we should show respect for other peoples and the natural world.

Chicago and culture – for many people who have never been to this city these two concepts do not seem to belong together. And yet Chicago can boast a very large and lively cultural scene. The classical music of the Chicago Symphony Orchestra also helps justify this reputation and it has been honoured with a Grammy award. Over 60 professional theatre groups work in the city, not necessarily any the worse for being in the Off-Loop, outside the city centre, since many a star has made the grade after working in a small suburban ensemble. Of course, such Broadway productions as "Chorus Line" and "Cats" have appeared in Chicago. The city is also famous for its museums and art galleries. The best known, most comprehensive and interesting and at the same time probably the largest tourist attraction in the city is the Museum of Science and Industry, a gigantic building in which visitors can both wonder at and actually experience the miracles of science and technology. You can explore a coal mine, watch a chick emerge from the egg, play with a computer, walk through the five metre-high model of a human heart, clamber through a German Second World War U-boat, explore the Apollo 8 capsule and watch a robot at work.

Chicago, the "Windy City". The city with broad shoulders. Glittering and thoroughly honest. American. Dedicated to progress and always a step ahead of the rest of America.

Marina City from the 1960s

Lofty skyscrapers. Museums and theatres. Gourmet restaurants and luxury hotels. The Chicago Bulls and the Chicago Cubs. But above all a city of many surprises. Open-air classical concerts in Grant Park. Indians walking along Devon Avenue. Travelling on the "El" through the ever-growing suburbs. Shopping in River North and Armitage Avenue. Important matches played on the legendary Wrigley Field. These are just some of the many different aspects to be found in Chicago. Or as Mark Twain once wrote: "It is impossible to keep pace with this city. It outlives its own prophecies and is always offering something new". Frank Lloyd Wright, the great architect, said about the city: "Some day Chicago will be the last beautiful city in the world".

Exploring the city

A city full of meaning: skyscrapers and old houses,
multiform districts and art on every street corner

The whole of Chicago is just a cloud – if you happen to pick a bad day and look out over the rain from Sears Tower or the Hancock Observatory. But when the weather is good the view is unforgettable, and the giant city lies at your feet in all its glory. Anyone who has ever stood on the Empire State Building in New York knows what a fine view is like. Chicago is more varied, architecturally more interesting, and this can be appreciated from high up. The gilded spire of the Carbide and Carbon Buildings towering up out of the sea of houses like a champagne bottle, the dainty ornamentation on the Wrigley Building, the palatial museums on the bank of Lake Michigan.

To get to know the true character of this city you should view it from above before plunging into the hurly-burly below. On the underground, in the trains of the dilapidated "El", in the bustle

Chicago is proud of its neo-Gothic Historic Water Tower which survived the Great Fire of 1871

of State Street, on the squares in front of the high-rise towers and banks, on the Magnificent Mile north of the Chicago River, on the banks of Lake Michigan, in such suburbs as Chinatown and Pilsen. "The best things in life are free" say the Americans, and that is certainly the case in Chicago. Anyone who goes through the city with his eyes open and simply allows himself to drift along with the crowds of local people need not spend a cent and yet will experience the genuine, true Chicago and sometimes the Windy City too. For it is windy along Lake Michigan and anyone coming to Chicago when it is raining or in winter will truly have little to laugh about.

But when the sun shines Chicago is a delight. For what was formerly the pork butchery of the world and a "blue collar" city has now become a metropolis *par excellence*. Chicago surprises its visitors with what it can offer in the way of various forms of culture and chic shopping streets, world-famous museums and first-class restaurants.

MARCO POLO SELECTION: SIGHTSEEING

1 John Hancock Observatory
Fantastic view with gimmicks
(page 14)

2 John G. Shedd Aquarium
It is even more beautiful
underwater! (page 29)

3 Lincoln Park
Tigers hide in this park by
the side of the lake
(pages 16 and 29)

4 Wrigley Field
But only when there is a
baseball match!
(page 21)

5 Chicago Loop
Chicago live, pure Chicago!
(page 24)

6 Old Town
Relax in a street café
(page 25)

7 Magnificent Mile
The "in" shopping street
(page 26)

8 Lake Michigan
The lake without banks –
like the seaside (page 19)

9 Chicago Board of Trade
The most beautiful
skyscraper (page 27)

**10 Chicago Architecture
Foundation**
Skyscrapers with plenty of
knowledgeable guides
(page 20)

It is impossible to do this city justice in just a few days, in fact you cannot see everything in four weeks. Therefore do not try to rush from one place of interest to another. Choosing what to see adds spice to the visit. Just one day can be an experience if you limit yourself to a view from the Hancock Observatory, spend your lunch break in front of the James R. Thompson Center, visit the Museum of Science and Industry and spend a pleasant evening in a "blues" club. Experience Chicago with all its character, really see the city, listen, smell and taste it; on a skyscraper or on the banks of Lake Michigan, under the elevated railway or in the Loop, at a hot-dog stand or on Navy Pier, one of the most interesting cities in North America is waiting just for you.

VANTAGE POINTS

John Hancock Center Observatory (109/D 1)

★ From the observatory on the 94th floor, lavishly renovated in 1997, there is a superb view over the sea of houses below and of Lake Michigan. The strong wind really makes itself felt on the fenced-in viewing platform – not for those who are afraid of heights! The new attractions following the most recent renovation include the "speaking telescope" (it offers commentary in English, Spanish, French and Japanese) with sound effects, and a *history wall* which provides information on the city's history. In the ticket lobby there is an exhibition about the building of the skyscraper. What is said to be the world's fastest elevator takes just 40 seconds to reach the observatory. *Open daily 9 am–midnight, admission US$ 7, 875 N. Michigan, Near North, buses 145, 146, 147, 151, subway Red Line to Chicago/State*

Lake Shore Drive (109–111/E 1–6)
This main artery through the city centre, also designated "Outer Drive" and "US Highway 41" on some road maps, is worth driving along at night, when it is not so busy and you can enjoy a fine view of the illuminated skyline and Buckingham Fountain shimmering in all its multicoloured splendour. The most beautiful section is that between Grand Avenue and Wacker Drive, near Fullerton Avenue, and north of Hyde Park.

Michigan Avenue Bridge (109/D 3)
The perfect spot from which to take a night-time photograph of the illuminated skyline. Tribune Tower and the Wrigley Building gleam under floodlights. The French trapper Louis Jolliet, after whom a small town was named, and the Jesuit priest Marquette were the first white men to cross the river at this point in 1873, followed eight years later by the explorer La Salle en route to the Mississippi.

Sears Tower (108/B 5)
Even though Petronas Towers in Kuala Lumpur is now taller, this black tower with its dark windows, comprising 110 storeys and standing 430 m high, is still one of the most impressive skyscrapers anywhere in the world. From 1973 to 1996 Sears

Tower was the world's tallest building. This massive tower owes its stability to a fixed concrete platform and nine steel rods 23 metres thick which go right to the top – a design by the top architect Bruce Graham who worked for the firm of Skidmore, Owings and Merrill. Visitors are put in the picture by means of a rather boring video before the 70 second journey to the Skydeck on the 103rd floor begins. From there you have a panoramic view of the rooftops of Chicago and of the surrounding countryside. In the foyer stands the "Universe" sculpture by Alexander Calder. *Open daily 9 am–11 pm, until 10 pm in winter, admission US$ 8, 233 S. Wacker Dr., west of the Loop, buses 1, 7, 126, 146, 151, 156 or El Brown, Orange to Quincy*

LIBRARIES

Harold Washington Library Center (109/D 6)
This brick building with angels blowing trumpets (the "Windy City") is also an architectural delight, especially the spectacular Winter Garden. However, the books are the real attraction. No other public library in the USA has such a large selection. For visitors with little time (or desire) for studying the temporary exhibitions there are some interesting events and lectures. A programme can be obtained on *Tel, 312/747 43 00, Open Mon 9 am–7 pm, Tue, Thu 11 am–7 pm, Fri, Sat 9 am–5 pm, Sun 1–5 pm, guided tours 10 am and 2 pm, 400 State Street, buses 11, 145, 146, 147, North Side, El Brown, Orange to Harold Washington Library Center*

Graceland Cemetery (O)

Graceland Cemetery, without doubt the city's finest cemetery, was laid out in 1860 and lies in the shadow of the apartments on Clark Street. At that time there were only a few public parks in the USA, and so cemeteries had a dual role to fulfil; they were a resting place for the deceased and somewhere for the living to come to relax. Numerous celebrities lie buried here including the architect Ludwig Mies van der Rohe, who from 1938 onwards designed a number of high-rise buildings in Chicago and New York. Other people buried here who left their mark on the city are: George Pullman, the manufacturer of luxury railway coaches, the private detective Allen Pinkerton, Marshall Field who founded the department store, and the co-founder of the American baseball league, William A. Hulbert, whose gravestone is (naturally) topped by a baseball. *Open daily until dusk, 4001 N. Clark St., North Side, El Brown to Irving Park*

Rosehill Cemetery (O)

A tranquil cemetery since 1859 in North Side and the last resting place of several hundred soldiers of the American Civil War. Every year a ceremony is held in honour of those who fought in this bloody encounter. Julius Rosenwald, the founder of the Museum of Science and Industry, and John G. Shedd, founder of the aquarium which bears his name, also lie buried here. *5800 N. Rosewood Av., North Side, bus 49B, El Brown to Western Avenue*

Chicago Botanic Garden (O)

Twenty gardens, one name: the Chicago Botanic Garden is so large that visitors are transported through the magnificent blooms in a small train. Its attractions include the *English Walled and Rose Gardens*, which could well grace the front of an English palace, the *Japanese Islands* with their unconventional and manicured Japanese gardens, the prolifically productive *Fruit and Vegetable Garden*, the *Waterfall Garden* and the *Prairie Demonstration Garden* in which the flora reflects and illustrates the prairies. *Open daily 8 am until sunset, guided tours US$ 3.50, 1000 Lake Cook Rd., Glencoe (30 minutes north of the city), suburban train to Glencoe*

Grant Park (109/E 4–111/E 6)

❖ Of all people, it was A. Montgomery Ward, the legendary department store king, who prevented this area on Lake Michigan from being built upon. We have his initiative to thank for the development of this 130 ha park with extensive lawns east of Michigan Avenue. In summer Grant Park is the venue for numerous concerts and events, with classical music being performed in the Petrillo Music Shell on the corner of Jackson Boulevard and Columbus Drive. The most striking feature in the park is the *Buckingham Fountain*, built in 1926 and modelled on one at Versailles. *Buses 3, 4, 6, 146, 151 to Michigan Avenue*

Lincoln Park (107/D–E 1–4)

★ ❖ ✿ The largest (and, above all, longest) park in the city lies along the edge of Lake Michigan between North and Ardmore Avenues. It was beautifully laid out in the 1870s on the site of the former municipal cemetery. The statue of the famous president after whom it was named was the work of Augustus Saint-Gaudens. The park contains beaches, marinas and a variety of sporting activities including a golf course. Also in the park is one of the largest and most popular municipal zoos in the country, and the Lincoln Park Conservatory which has a large collection of exotic plants. In addition there are two museums. Numerous walkways and cycle paths run through the park which is also a favourite spot for joggers. *Buses 22, 145, 146, 147, 151, 156*

Osaka Garden (O)

A traditional Japanese garden behind the Museum of Science and Industry, a gift from the Japanese government at the World Exhibition of 1893. *Open daily, 5900 S. Lake Shore Dr., Hyde Park, bus 10 to the Museum of Science and Industry*

HISTORIC BUILDINGS

Historic Water Tower (109/D 1)
The Historic Water Tower is one of the few buildings which survived the fire of 1871 and became a symbol of the "it's now or never" spirit shown by the citizens who within a few months had built a new city centre and made Chicago the fastest-growing US metropolis of the 19th century. This pseudo-Gothic tower was built in 1869 by William W. Boyington, a major architect whose Revival Style influenced the building of many commercial buildings in Chicago. His work was also in demand after the fire. In fact the 50 metre-tall Water Tower was not an important building. Its only function was to stabilise the flow of water from the neighbouring pumping station. But its symbolic worth remains

Festivals are often celebrated around the Buckingham Fountain in summer

17

undiminished to this day and makes it one of Chicago's major attractions, *800 N. Michigan Av., Magnificent Mile, buses 11, 66, 145, 146, 147, 151, El Red to Chicago Street*

Robie House (O)
Ambitious design with emphasis on the horizontal and projecting features are the hallmarks of the so-called Prairie school of architecture which is supposedly reminiscent of the American Middle West and was developed by the legendary architect Frank Lloyd Wright. The best example of this somewhat sober style is Robie House, built in 1909 on Woodlawn Avenue. A part of the building has been renovated and is open to the public. *Admission US$ 8, tours Mon–Fri 11 am, 1 pm and 3 pm, Sat, Sun half-hourly 11 am–3.30 pm, Hyde Park, 5757 S. Woodlawn Av., bus 55*

CHURCHES & PLACES OF WORSHIP

Baha'i Temple (O)
Architecturally related to the Taj Mahal and therefore one of the most spectacular places of worship in Chicago or its surroundings. Louise Bourgeois designed this magnificent white edifice which is surrounded by well-tended gardens and was built for adherents to the Baha'i faith. The members of this church believe in the unification of all religious demoninations and beliefs. *Visitor centre open daily in summer 10 am–10 pm, in winter daily 10 am–5 pm, temple daily from 7 am, 100 Linden Av., Wilmette (c. 40 minutes north of the city), El Purple Express to Linden*

Quinn Chapel (113/D 3)
A Victorian church of the Afro-American population, since 1847 the oldest black community in the city. The Quinn Chapel African Methodist Episcopal Church was founded during the Civil War, Even Martin Luther King Jr. preached here. *2401 S. Wabash Av., South Side, bus 29 to 24th Street*

Rockefeller Memorial Chapel (O)
Without John D. Rockefeller's "small change" there would have been no University of Chicago, sang the students at its opening. He donated more than 35 million dollars to the university which was founded in 1890. The neo-Gothic chapel which now bears his name is a monumental building designed by Bertram G. Goodhue, the architect of the Empire State Building in New York. Above the altar is a circular stained glass window, and the world's second largest carillon accompanies the frequent concerts. The building is open to visitors. *Concerts during term-time: Wed 12.15 pm, Thu 7.30 pm, during the summer holidays (June–Aug): Sun 4 pm, open to visitors daily 8 am–4 pm, 5850 S. Woodlawn Av., buses 6, 55*

Unity Temple (O)
The place of worship of the Unitarian Universalist Church is a perfect example of the effectiveness of the Prairie House style adopted by Frank Lloyd Wright. The architect was obliged to work to a minimal budget and to use reinforced concrete blocks. In the sober interior of the church you feel protected from the world outside; the congregation stands near the preacher and

pass him as they leave the church. The side entrance is intended to create a private sphere. Also of interest is the geometric design of the amber-coloured windows which diffuse a strange light during the service. *Guided tours US$ 6, daily 10 am–5 pm, in winter Mon–Fri midday–4 pm, Sat, Sun 10 am–5 pm, guided tours Sat, Sun hourly 1–3 pm, admission US$ 4, 875 Lake St., Oak Park, El Green to Harlem*

PLANETARIUM

Adler Planetarium   (111/F 4)
The Adler Planetarium on the shores of Lake Michigan is a twelve-sided granite building with a copper dome. It was founded and opened in 1930 by Max Adler, a leading employee of the department store chain of Sears and Roebuck. The "Journey to Infinity" in the StarRider Theater is an incredible high-tech operation. More than 150 projectors produce magically impressive special effects in a man-made firmament, the onlooker is interactively involved as if in a huge computer game and decides the route of the space journey. The development of astronomy is portrayed on three floors with the help of antique telescopes and other exhibits. The space travel exhibition includes a space suit and genuine Mars rock. Close-up photographs of the moon and other heavenly bodies can be seen on a monitor. The Planetarium can be experienced virtually through the internet *(www.adlerplanetarium,org)*. *Admission US$ 5, free on Tue, StarRider Theater $ 5, Mon–Thu 9 am–5*

pm, Fri 9 am–9 pm, Sat, Sun 9 am–6 pm, in summer Sat–Wed 9 am–6 pm, Thu, Fri 9 am–9 pm, 1300 S, Lake Shore Dr., east of the Loop, buses 6, 10, 12, 130, 146

RADIO & TELEVISION STUDIO

Talk shows
Oprah Winfrey, the USA chat show queen, is one of the richest and most influential women in America. In her shows she interviews great stars such as Michael Jackson and Leonardo diCaprio. The centre of the Oprah Winfrey empire lies in Chicago and her shows are filmed there also. Anyone wishing to obtain one of the few tickets available to be in the audience must telephone to reserve one at least two months beforehand: *Tel. 312/591 92 22.* The show is filmed from September to May in the Harpo Studios *(1058 W. Washington St.)*.

LAKE

Lake Michigan
★✪The Chicago skyline is reflected in the waters of one of the Great Lakes, and also in winter when an icy wind whistles across the lake. Without Lake Michigan the city would be only half as beautiful. Those who know Chicago take advantage of the few sunny summer days to spend time on one of the beaches or in a boat on the lake. The plain statistics relating to Lake Michigan are also impressive: 494 km long, 190 km wide, maximum depth nearly 300 m, length of shoreline 2,635 km. ✌ The finest views of

Tourists love the "Untouchable Tours" which follow in the footsteps of Al Capone

the lake are to be had from Navy Pier, from Shedd Aquarium and (of course) from one of the numerous pleasure boats.

SIGHTSEEING TOURS

Chicago Architecture Foundation (109/D 1)

★ This company offers more than 60 guided tours, all of which cover the unique architecture of Chicago. Expert guides know the stories of the historic buildings down to the smallest detail and also have plenty of anecdotes to tell. The company arranges exhibitions, lectures and other programmes dealing with Chicago architecture. *Mon–Fri 9 am–7 pm, Sat 9.30 am–7 pm, Sun 9.30–6 pm, prices vary, 224 S. Michigan Av., Magnificent Mile, buses 60, 151, El Green, Orange, Purple to Adams St., there is a second tour centre in the John Hancock Center, 875 N. Michigan Av., buses 145, 146, 147, 151, subway Red Line to Chicago St.*

A few selected tours:

Architecture River Cruise; A tour lasting one and a half hours, considered by experts as the best tour offered by this company because it combines interesting information with superb panoramic views of the skyline. The guides are renowned for their brief but informative talks. *May–Oct daily, ticket US$ 18, Michigan Av. Bridge, buses 2, 3, 10, 145, 146, 147, 150, 151 to Wacker Drive*

Chicago Duck Tours: Brightly-painted amphibious vehicles, ducks, transport you across Lake Michigan and the city centre streets. The only vehicles which are at home in both elements, they can thus provide fundamentally different views of the city. *Information: Tel. 312/461 11 33*

Loop Tour Train: This tour takes you on a journey of architectural discovery in an elevated railway train. Every Saturday the company's guides take you on a forty minute tour of the city centre. *Free tickets from the Visitor Information Center/Chicago Cultural Center, 77 E. Randolph St. The El trip starts at Randolph/Wabash Station on the Brown Line.*

The Spirit of Chicago (109/F 3)
↘↗ Sightseeing tours and entertaining dinner cruises across Lake Michigan, with evening meal and cabaret. The view of the evening Chicago skyline is breathtaking. *Daily, tickets US$ 31–37 (lunch tours), US$ 56–73 (dinner tours), Navy Pier, 600 E. Grand Av., buses 29, 56, 65, 66, 120, 121, El Red to Grand/State, free trolleybus from there*

Untouchable Tours (108/C 2–3)
You are taken through Chicago following in the footsteps of such legendary gangsters as Al Capone and to their strongholds of the wild 1930s. The guides travel in the coach with you dressed as gangsters and point out historic places such as O'Bannion's Flower Shop where the St Valentine's Day massacre took place. One of the most entertaining sightseeing tours. *The tours start from in front of Rock'n Roll McDonald's on the corner of Clark/Ohio St., Mon–Wed 10 am, Thu 10 am and 1 pm, Fri 10 am, 1 pm and 7.30 pm, Sat 10 am, 1 pm and 5 pm, Sun 11 am and 2 pm, tickets US$ 20, P.O. Box 43185, Chicago, IL 60643*

SPORTING VENUES

Wrigley Field (O)
★ ☺ Even though the Chicago Cubs have long since forgotten what it is like to win, because the Chicago Bears have taken over their mantle, baseball is an American tradition and Wrigley Field is a shrine for all fans. American football and basketball also have a strong following. Behind the ivy-covered walls of Wrigley Field all is still well with the world and the

Where the "Cubbies" are cheered on: Wrigley Field

true heart of America is beating. The advertising boards are still changed manually, high-tech is a foreign word even though the stadium is not short on comfort. *Games played from Apr to Oct, for details and dates: Tel. 312/404 28 27. Box office open Mon–Fri 9 am–6 pm, Sat. 9 am–4 pm as well as on match days, 1060 W. Addison St., subway Red Line to Addison*

Those who support the Chicago White Sox are well served at *Comiskey Park (333 W. 35th St.)*, while fans of the Bulls should go to the *United Center (1901 Madison St.)*.

CITY DISTRICTS

Chinatown (112/B 1–2)
Wentworth Avenue and Cermak Road are the busy main streets of the lively Chinese enclave south of the Loop. The first Cantonese came to Chicago before the First World War and settled in the quarter now known as Chinatown. Characteristics of the district include the wooden Chinatown Gate and the red

Chinatown, a piece of China south of the Loop

roofs of the pagodas as well as dim-sum restaurants, greengrocers' shops, tea dealers and bakeries. The decorated Chinese roofs often conceal plain brick houses which were built by other inhabitants, and scarcely differ from the uninteresting apartment houses of Hongkong Chinese immigrants. Visitors from the West find this district fascinating and are struck by the colourful hustle and bustle of the market people and the exotic smells, they also enjoy visiting the many restaurants. However, you would do well to ignore the garish kitch in the Chinese souvenir shops. Many of the items for sale are not worth buying. On the other side of Chinatown Gate lies the impressive *Pui Tak Center*, the hub of Chinese trade and commerce.

Gold Coast (107/E 4–5)
On the edge of the lake between Oak Street and North Avenue lies one of the city's most expensive residential areas. After the Great Fire the richest citizens settled here, hence the name. Today the scene is typified predominantly by high-rise apartments. Tourists seldom stray into this district unless they want to relax from the stress of sightseeing. The exception: *Oak Street Beach* between Lake Shore Drive and Lake Michigan. On Astor Street between Division Street and North Avenue some of the magnificent houses which were built after the Great Fire are still standing.

Hyde Park/University
☛ see map on page 24
The former suburb in the south of Chicago, modelled on a small town in New England in its

Relaxing on the Lakefront: Oak Street Beach

layout, has been absorbed by the city and now lies like an oasis in the shadow of the University of Chicago. On the university site and its surroundings park-like roads and residential areas with a European ambience predominate. Here can be found the world-famous Museum of Science and Industry. It is the only building remaining from the 1893 World Exhibition and provides an impression of that memorable and monumental event. When it was founded the University of Chicago was intended as a rival to Harvard and Yale. It did indeed produce more than 60 Nobel Prize winners, but it never attained the same legendary reputation as the other colleges. Its buildings are reminiscent of English universities, especially *International House*, a meeting place for international students, and *Ida Noyes Hall* with its giant library. In the immediate vicinity may be found some houses designed by the architect Frank Lloyd Wright including Robie House, now occupied by the Institute of International Studies.

Lincoln Park/Lakeview (O)
The city's best residential district lies east of Lincoln Park. Between Lincoln Avenue and Halsted Street are some of the best restaurants and bars in the city. Some "Off-Loop" theatres have established themselves near DePaul University. Lakeview became home to numerous gays and lesbians and has the resultant clubs. The area surrounding Wrigley Field, a tasteful residential quarter, has been named Wrigleyville.

Little Italy (O)
Italian is spoken to the west of the University of Illinois at Chicago. In Taylor Street and the surrounding streets most of the inhabitants are descendants of Italian immigrants who came from Tuscany some decades ago. As regards architecture and places of interest this quarter has little to offer, but those wishing to savour the Italian atmosphere

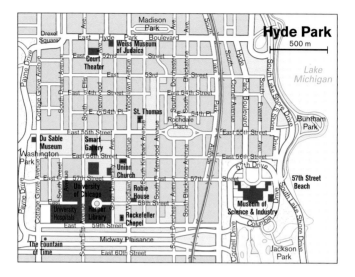

or dine in true Italian style during their holiday will find the right places to go here. Countless restaurants and street cafés exude a Mediterranean atmosphere. Almost cult status has been bestowed on *Mario's Italian Lemonade (1070 W. Taylor St.)*, where, as the name implies, Mario and his friends dispense their lemonade.

The Loop (108–109/C–D 4–6)

★ ☀ A synonym for Chicago's financial and business district, which has long since spread beyond the Loop as a result of the elevated railway and is now bordered by the Chicago River in the north and west, Michigan Avenue in the east and Roosevelt Avenue in the south. But the heart of the city still beats here in the Loop, in Marshall Field's, at Carson Pirie Scott's and in the shops in busy State Street, in the Financial District, in the Art Institute of Chicago and with the Chicago Symphony Orchestra and the Lyric Opera of Chicago, in the Harold Washington Library Center and the numerous restaurants. To get to know the real Chicago you should mingle with the passers-by on State Street; only during the rush hour (too much traffic) and at night (crime) should you avoid the Loop.

North Town/Andersonville (O)

Ethnic minorities and immigrants who came to Chicago during recent years have settled in the northern part of the city. The area around Argyle Street and North Clark Street is dominated by Chinese and Vietnamese, and to the north of it Scandinavian immigrants live in Andersonville. This little township is very peaceful and the small shops selling Scandinavian arts and crafts are worth a visit. *Rogers Park*, formerly a Jewish community, has become home to Asians, Indians and Russians.

Old Town   (106–107/D 4–5)
★ West of North Dearborn Street, on North Wells between Division Street and North Avenue, lies Old Town, an area of about 3 sq km and the city's entertainment quarter. North Avenue was originally known as "German Broadway", because many German immigrants settled there around 1840. German tradition was maintained with the famous Oscar Meyer Sausage Factory, a brewery and a piano manufactory. Today just a few clubs remain as a reminder of its German past, because after the Depression mainly artists from other nations settled in the quarter but there are still a number of streets named after German writers. During the 1960s and 1970s Old Town became home to the "flower power" cult. Today the Victorian houses are occupied mainly by high earners with boutiques, souvenir shops, restaurants and bars, and the theatres and clubs provide evening entertainment.

Pilsen   (O)
Before the Second World War this district north of West Cermak Road was popular with Bohemian immigrants. Today only the red-brick houses and the district's name remain to remind us of the Bohemians, and for some years mainly Spanish has been heard on West 18th Street and it may well not be long before "Pilsen" is replaced by "Little Mexico". Only in a fast-living place like Chicago can a city district change its identity so rapidly.

Pilsen is a genuine artists' quarter. On Halsted Street, between 18th and 19th Streets, artists meet in a concealed rear courtyard with a beautiful garden. In September each year, during *Pilsen Artists' Open House*, they open up their studios to the public. The area is best avoided in the evenings. The elevated railway station on 18th Street is a work of art in itself; unknown artists have decorated the walls with paintings with a pre-Columbian feel. Similar murals can be admired at the *Orozco Community Academy (1439 W. 18th Street)*. Naturally, the restaurants in Pilsen are all owned by Mexicans.

River North   (108–109/C–D 2–3)
On the other side of the Magnificent Mile, in the west of Ontario Street and the streets surrounding it, lies a former warehouse district which – like SoHo in New York – has been made into a chic area with art galleries, antique shops, small restaurants and cafés. Artists and others to whom it appeals reside in converted attic apartments and meet with other "in" people by lantern light.

Wicker Park/Bucktown   (O)
Hip and more hip, that is Wicker Park. The former working man's quarter, lying to the west of Gold Coast district, was settled by Germans and Poles in the late 19th century, was then discovered by artists and for a few years now has been the ultimate "in" scene.

A multitude of artists and would-be artists settled here, followed by the inevitable coffee houses, the visible sign in the USA that an area is really up to date. Hypermodern restaurants and cult clubs give it an artistic touch, much to the regret of the genuine freelance residents who have lived here for some decades. In September each year, during the festival known as "Around the Coyote", many studios hold an open day. The district's best known building is the *Flat Iron Building* with its numerous studios and galleries.

STREETS

Magnificent Mile   (109/D 1-3)

★ North Michigan Avenue, the stretch between the bridge over the Chicago River and Oak Street being known as the *Magnificent Mile*, marks the most elegant quarter of Downstream Chicago. Here you can find numerous galleries, boutiques and luxury shops. On this boulevard, one of the finest in the USA, trends are set or imported from Europe, people sip their cappuccino or expresso or go window shopping if their purses will not stretch to the outrageous prices. Here can be found some of the most expensive hotels, restaurants and boutiques.

Printer's Row   (108/C 6)

From 1880 to 1950 Dearborn Street, south of Jackson Boulevard, was the centre of the printing industry. Printed and unprinted paper was taken to Dearborn Station by way of Plymouth Court and Federal Street. By 1950 Congress Street had been widened and paper was transported by lorry along the new freeway. The oldest railway station in Chicago was

converted to a shopping centre and studios and luxury dwellings replaced the old warehouses. Its smart restaurants and shops make the former Printer's Row an interesting alternative to Gold Coast and Old Town.

ENTERTAINMENT

Disney Quest   (109/D 3)

♣ A virtual amusement park in the middle of the city. There are four sections in which kids of the "new generation" can let off steam to their heart's content in artificial computer worlds. In the *Explore Zone* they can visit Hades with Hercules or go on a virtual journey of discovery through the jungle in rubber dinghies; in the *Score Zone* they try to win points in new 3-D worlds; in the *Create Zone* they use their imagination, while the *Replay Zone* is a colourful annual market for computer kids. *55 East Ohio St., Magnificent Mile, buses 3, 140, 151, subway Red Line to Chicago St.*

Navy Pier   (109/F 3)

♣Navy Pier was built during the First World War, and in the Second World War was a training centre for marine pilots. Over recent years this area has been redeveloped at great expense. In 1995 it was made into a leisure centre with restaurants, shops and roundabouts. Palm trees and flowers flourish under a glass dome, while beautiful fountains play. The 15 storey-high giant wheel was modelled on the original from the 1893 exhibition. Other attractions include a skating rink, an IMAX cinema, a high-tech McDonald's and the Skyline Stage for open-air concerts. From the pier there is a breathtaking view of Chicago's skyline. *Open Sun–Thu 10 am–10 pm, Fri, Sat 10 am–midnight, in winter Mon–Sat 10 am–10 pm, Sun 10 am–7 pm, 600 E. Grand Av., buses 29, 56, 65, 66, 120, 121, El Red to Grand/State, free trolleybus from there*

SKYSCRAPERS

Carbide and Carbon Building (109/D 4)

This, the city's most impressive art deco skyscraper, towers up from its black granite foundations. Its outer walls are clad in dark green terracotta, the top decorated with gold leaf. It is said that the Burnham Brothers, who designed this edifice in 1929, were inspired by a champagne bottle wrapped in gold leaf. *230 N. Michigan Av., Loop, bus 3 to S. Water Street*

Chicago Board of Trade (108/C 6)

★ The Stock Exchange has been housed since 1930 in one of the city's most beautiful skyscrapers. Because in the 19th century the exchange dealt mainly in the corn trade Ceres, the Greek goddess of agriculture, looks down from the top of the building. From the visitor centre on the fifth floor there is a view of the hectic hustle and bustle of the city centre. The mysterious hand signals used by the stockbrokers are explained in a brochure. Even more impressive than the trading in shares is the building itself. Dainty art deco motifs adorn the skyscraper which incorporates a modern extension built by the architect Helmut Jahn in 1980. *Open Mon–Fri 8 am–2 pm, 141 W.*

Modern art on Navy Pier

Jackson Bldv., Loop, buses 1, 7, 60, 126, 151, 156 or El Brown, Orange to Jackson

Chicago Tribune Tower (109/D 3)

The Chicago Tribune has an architectural competition to thank for its imposing publishing building. Raymond Hood and John Mead Howells won it and designed the 46 storeyed neo-Gothic edifice on Michigan Avenue which is rather reminiscent of a massive church. The outer wall incorporates stones from some of the world's most famous buildings, including the Berlin Wall, the Pyramid of Cheops in Egypt, the Colossus in Rome, the Great Wall of China, Westminster Abbey in London and St Peter's Cathedral in Rome. The front pages of important editions of the Chicago Tribune are on display in the foyer. They contain reports on the Great Fire in Chicago and the entry of the USA into the Second World War. The WGN radio station, an institution in Chicago, broadcasts live from the lobby. *Open daily during the day, 435 N. Michigan Av., Magnificent Mile, buses 3, 11, 29, 65, 147, 151, 157, subway Red Line to Grand*

James R. Thompson Centre (108/C 4)

To date this former State of Illinois Center remains one of Chicago's most controversial modern buildings. The daring design was by the world-famous German architect Helmut Jahn and was passed in spite of resistance from many official sources. The skyscraper now houses numerous offices. Helmut Jahn said "It was a miracle that I was able to bring this building to fruition". The main objections were in regard to the colour scheme: brilliant red, orange and silver dominate in this giant edifice of steel and glass, and the breathtaking illuminated courtyard, which goes right up to the 17th floor where it forms a cylindrical crown, gives the visitor the impression that he is in a space ship or a space station. The building was named after a long-serving governor of the state of Illinois. *100 W. Randolph St., Loop, subway/El Blue, Brown, Orange to Clark/Lake Street*

Marquette Building (108/C 5)

This E-shaped building, typical of the Chicago style of early Chicago, was designed by William Holabird and Martin Roche. Both architects were responsible for numerous buildings in the city around 1900. The wide windows allow daylight into all the rooms. Elaborate reliefs above the main doorway and mosaics on the marble walls of the foyer portray the life of the explorer Jacques Marquette who was the first white man to report on the region in which Chicago now lies. The building was named after him. *140 S. Dearborn, Loop, buses 60, 130, 151, subway/El Blue to Monroe*

Merchandise Mart (108/B 3)

Erected in 1931, this building has little to offer architecturally, but it is known beyond the city limits as the city's largest warehouse. Only the Pentagon can exceed it in area. Originally it was intended that only goods belonging to the department store king Marshall Field should be stored here, but since then shops, cafés and restaurants have established themselves on the two lower floors and furniture is stored above. In the entrance hall brightly coloured murals portray the trading nations of the world. *Between Wells and Franklin St., west of the Loop, El Brown to Merchandise Mart*

Monadnock Building (108/C 6)

Around the start of the twentieth century the mighty Monadnock Building was the largest office building in the world. The northern half of the sixteen-storeyed edifice was built of massive bricks and derided in a technical journal of the day as a giant chimney, while the southern half was built on a steel frame. The architects – untypically for the period – used no ornamentation of any kind, intending it to be just a sober office building. The southern half with its steel frame was used as a model for countless skyscrapers of the *art deco* era. *53 W. Jackson Blvd., Loop, buses 60, 130, 151, subway Blue, Red Lines to Jackson*

The Rookery   (108/C 5)
The building gets its name from the town hall which once stood here and in which birds nested after the Great Fire of 1871. The eleven-storeyed edifice, a skyscraper at the time. was completed in 1888. The famous architect Frank Lloyd Wright renovated the lobby in 1907. On the exterior are some striking Roman and Moorish motifs and dainty art deco ornamentation, while the large-scale and effective architecture of Wright predominates in the interior. In 1922 the Rookery was again renovated in the course of which the original decoration was revealed. *Open during the day, 209 La Salle St., Loop, buses 1, 22, 60, 151, El Brown and Orange to Quincy*

ZOOLOGICAL GARDENS

John G. Shedd Aquarium (111/E 4)
★ A coral reef in the middle of Chicago: sharks, barracudas and a plethora of multi-coloured fish frolic in the rivers and lakes in what is probably the largest covered aquarium in the world. The artificial sea lies in an octagonal marble building and boasts an impressive underwater world. Divers feed the fish on the Caribbean Reef and explain the characteristics of the marine creatures. The basin, which contains eleven million litres of sea water, appears almost unreal when viewed against the background of Lake Michigan which can be seen through large windows in the new Oceanarium. Beluga whales, dolphins, sea otters and sea lions from American waters frolic in the salt water. The characters and way of life of the sea creatures is explained by means of numerous exhibitions. *Admission US$ 10, open daily 9 am–6 pm, until 9 pm on Thu, in winter Mon–Fri 9 am–5 pm, Sat, Sun 9 am–6 pm, 1200 S. Lakeshore Dr., Near South, buses 6, 10, 12, 130, 146 to Michigan Avenue*

Lincoln Park Zoo   (107/D 1–2)
★ Free admission and open all year round – that is the case only in the Lincoln Park Zoo, one of the finest and largest zoological gardens in the USA. More than a thousand mammals, birds and reptiles live in the imaginatively designed enclosures, as well as elephants, gorillas, rhinos and big cats. Since 1997 some small members of endangered species have found a safe haven in the Small Mammal-Reptile House. *Admission free, Mon–Fri 10 am–5 pm, Sat, Sun 10 am–7 pm, until 5 pm in winter, 2200 N. Cannon Dr., Lincoln Park, buses 151, 156 to Lincoln Park*

Two hours in a museum

Chicago as a centre of world-famous museums – from legendary museums of science and industry to the small but excellent Ukrainian National Museum

The World Exhibition of 1893 already showed how proud the people of Chicago were of achievements in art, science and technology. At the time they celebrated the (supposed) superiority of the human mind with a monumental festival and also when building their renowned museums they showed that they were anything but modest and retiring: the Museum of Science and Industry, the Field Museum of Natural History and the Art Institute of Chicago, the city's three major museums, are all housed in sumptuous classical buildings.

Chicago is unquestionably a museum city which, in the eyes of many visitors, is higher up the scale than New York because its museums cover a wider range and are more lovingly designed. Interactive is the magic word. The "hands up" of the gangster

A magnificent classic edifice and an interactive place of learning: the Museum of Science and Industry

era has become "hands on". In Chicago's museums everything (almost) can be touched, and the visitor is let into the secrets of science and technology in a relaxed and active manner. You can learn about all the fields of knowledge on display in all their aspects and using the latest methods – a paradise especially for children who are not just tolerated but are actually welcomed in these museums.

As well as those described in detail in this guide we must also mention the following gems:

In the *Chicago Atheneum Museum of Architecture and Design (6 N. Michigan Av., Open Tue–Sat 11 am–6 pm. Sun 11 am–5 pm, admission US$ 3)* the ornamentation of historic buildings and modern architectural designs are portrayed and explained; in the *International Museum of Surgical Science (1524 N. Lake Shore Dr., Open Tue–Sat 10 am–4 pm, admission free)* surgical instruments are on display; in the new *National Vietnam Veterans Art Museum (1801 S. Indiana Av., Open Tue–Fri 11 am–6 pm,*

Sat 10 am–5 pm, Sun 11 am–5 pm, admission US$ 4) veterans of the Vietnam War display their impressive works of art which were often used as a form of therapy; in the *Peace Museum (314 W. Institute Place, Open Tue, Wed, Fri, Sat 11 am–5 pm, Thu midday–5 pm, admission US$ 4)* the universal theme is Peace. Original manuscripts by the protest singer Joan Baez and finally John Lennon's guitar are on display, and the *Swedish-American Museum Center (5211 N. Clark St., Open Tue–Fri 10 am–4 pm, Sat, Sun 10 am–3 pm, admission US$ 4)* pays homage to the cultural contribution made by Swedish immigrants.

A notable feature of all museums in Chicago is that admission is free on one day in the week. The disadvantage is that that is when they are most crowded.

American Police Center and Museum   (110/C 6)

Things were particularly difficult for the Chicago police during the 1960s. Violent demonstrations against the war in Vietnam and race riots shook the city. These serious troubles led some of the friends and relatives of policemen to found this little museum. In order to provide a better understanding of the work of the police, uniforms, equipment and other exhibits from the past and those relating to law enforcement are exhibited. The weapons on display include a sawn-off shotgun owned by Al Capone. There is a *memorial corner* in memory of police officers who lost their lives in the course of duty. A new feature is an exhibition on the history of women in the police force. *Open Mon–Fri 9.30 am–4.30 pm, admission US$ 4, 1717 S. State St., South Side buses 29, 44, 62, 164 to 18th Street*

The Art Institute of Chicago   (109/D 5)

★ Two bronze lions by the American sculptor Edward L. Kemeys guard the main entrance

Entrance to the Art Institute, famous above all for its Impressionist collection

MARCO POLO SELECTION: MUSEUMS

1 The Art Institute of Chicago
For nearly a century the two bronze lions have guarded valuable works of art from two millenia (page 32)

2 Chicago Children's Museum
Play and learn – in a children's paradise (page 34)

3 Chicago Historical Society
Everything about the 1893 World Exhibition and the "pork butchers of the world" (page 34)

4 The Field Museum of Natural History
Sue, the largest T-Rex in the world, and other wonders of nature (page 34)

5 Museum of Contemporary Art
Experimental art since 1945 (page 36)

6 Museum of Science and Industry
The world's largest interactive museum – the most outstanding of all the Chicago museums (page 36)

to the renowned Art Institute which was built on the occasion of the 1893 World Exhibition and has been renovated again and again, the last time being in 1987. Leading businessmen had decided to show the city's cultural treasures to the world. The Chicago architects Daniel Burnham and John Wellborn Root were asked to design it but Root died suddenly and Burnham was already engaged in designing the World Exhibition. So a Boston firm was appointed to construct this classical style building. An elegant staircase leads to the exhibition rooms.

On the second floor European art is arranged chronologically, from the Middle Ages to the Late Impressionists. Paintings and sculptures by renowned artists are displayed in spacious rooms and their full splendour is reflected in the daylight rays. Dutch masters such as Rembrandt, the Spaniard El Greco, but in particular great Impressionists like Renoir, Manet and Degas are represented by some well-known works. The museum also boasts the world's largest collection of Monet paintings. Other treasures in the Art Institute include Marc Chagall's colourful windows and Georgia O'Keefe's "Sky Above the Clouds", the largest painting in the museum. Modern art is represented by such names as Picasso, Grant Wood and Edward Hopper. Less crowded are the exhibitions of Asiatic African art and the photographs on the ground floor. There you can also find an *Education Center* for younger visitors. *Open Mon, Wed, Thu, Fri 10.30 am–4.30 pm, Tue 10.30 am–8 pm, Sat 10 am–5 pm, Sun midday–5 pm, admission*

US$ 8, Tue free, 111 S. Michigan Av., Grant Park, buses 3, 4, 60, 145, 147, 151, subway/El Green, Brown, Purple, Orange to Adams Street

Chicago Children's Museum (109/F 3)

★ ✻ Children can learn through play in this museum which is specially equipped for them and was moved to Navy Pier some years ago. Everything can be touched and handled by them. In the *Waterways* exhibition they can learn the importance and uses of water by building small dams, fashioning fountains and (of course!) getting thoroughly soaked in the process. On a three-decked sailing ship they can clamber around to their hearts' content. *Face to face: Dealing with Prejudice and Discrimination*, an impressive multimedia show, is intended to help youngsters form judgements of all kinds. *Playmaze* is a model town in which children under five can play. Adults who are still children at heart will be certain to enjoy this museum. To the north of the site *Jane Addams Park* and *Milton Lee Olive Park* are ideal for a quiet stroll or a rest. *Open Tue–Sun 10 am–5 pm, admission US$ 6, free Thu 5–8 pm, Navy Pier, 700 E. Grand Av., east of the Loop, buses 29, 56, 65, 66, 120, 121, El Red to Grand/State, free trolleybus from there*

Chicago Historical Society (107/D–E 4)

★ Not a dry and boring museum, as the name might suggest, but one that actually provides lively exhibitions on the history of Chicago and the USA.

The development of the city on Lake Michigan is followed from the time it was first founded as a post in the wilderness right up to the 20th century. There is documentary evidence of the pioneering spirit shown by the citizens of Chicago throughout its history. Moving events from the time when the country was first settled are portrayed in the documents headed "We the People; Creating a New Nation 1765–1820". Temporary exhibitions deal with everyday life during the pioneering period. *Open Mon–Sat 9.30 am–4.30 pm, Sun midday–5 pm, admission US$ 5, 1601 N. Clark St., Lincoln Park, buses 11, 22, 36, 72, 151, 156 to Lincoln Park*

DuSable Museum of African-American History (O)

☛ see map on page 24

Chicago, where almost a half of the population are of African descent, is just the sort of city that needs a museum like the DuSable, which portrays the history and culture of black Americans. The exhibition concentrates on the period between 1930 and 1970, especially on the cultural thrust after the Depression and the artistic revival of African culture in the 1960s. Jazz and blues concerts, readings and other events are held in the auditorium. *Open Mon–Sat 10 am–5 pm, Sunday midday–5 pm, admission US$ 3, free on Thu, Hyde Park, buses 3, 4, 55, subway Red Line to Washington Park*

The Field Museum of Natural History (111/E 4)

★ Natural history in abundance. Only a fraction of the 20 million

The Field Museum of Natural History houses exhibits from all over the world

and more items owned by the Field Museum is actually on display in this magnificent classical building designed by the architect Daniel Burnham. At the time of the 1893 World Exhibition the artifacts were still housed in what is now the Museum of Science and Industry. Since 1921 the Field Museum has ranked as one of the largest and most impressive museums in the world. The latest prize specimen is the skeleton of Sue, the world's largest dinosaur, which was discovered in South Dakota in 1990. The monster's skull alone weighs a ton!

Fresh light was thrown on the daily life and rites of the Egyptian pharaohs following the excavation of items from the tomb of Unis-Ankh, when even a market place of the period was reconstructed. Since the new millenium there has been an exhibition labelled "Underground Adventures", a journey into the miniature world which exists below the surface of the prairies of Illinois, whereby those watching get the impression thay they are shrinking to the size of beetles. *Open daily 9 am–5 pm, admission US$ 7, free on Wed, Roosevelt Rd. at Lakeshore Dr., Grant Park, buses 6, 10, 12, 130, 156 to the Museum*

Frank Lloyd Wright Home and Studio (**O**)

This simple dwelling, which the famous architect designed when he was only 22, is perhaps the best example of his artistic vision. In designing his own house and studio he did not have to consider the demands of a client. Between 1889 and 1909 he constantly changed the house just as he wished. His artistic glass constructions and bold geometric shapes astounded even his colleagues. Each room conformed to his ideals. The house and studio, including the furnishings and fittings, have remained just as they looked when he left in 1909. *Guided tours only, Mon–Fri 11 am, 1 and 3 pm, Sat, Sun 10 am, 3.30 pm, admission US$ 8, 951 Chicago Av., bus 23, Oak Park, subway Blue Line to Harlem*

Mexican Fine Arts Center Museum (O)

Mexican art in Pilsen, the quarter inhabited by Mexican immigrants. This exemplary museum displays the full range of Latin American art, from pre-Columbian statues of gods to young *avant garde* Mexican immigrants. Among the thousand and more objects which are displayed at present are paintings by such Mexican masters as Rivera, Orozco and Siqueiros, folk art by the Linares family and contemporary art by Carmen López Garza. The museum is associated with the "Day of the Dead", which begins in September and lasts eight weeks, with special exhibitions and programmes by its own radio station WRTE (90.5 FM). *Open daily except Mon 10 am–5 pm, admission free, 1852 W. 19th St., Pilsen, bus 9, subway Blue Line to 18th Street*

Museum of Contemporary Art (109/D 2)

★ There are divided opinions in Chicago regarding the sober façade and somewhat sombre appearance of the Museum of Contemporary Art – some critics compare it to the sort of museum found in a middle-sized town in Europe. Josef Paul Kleihues from Berlin (certainly not a middle-sized town) designed it in the early 1990s. However, there is no dispute regarding the various

exhibitions of modern art which have been held here continuously since 1945. More than 7,000 items by such well known artists as René, Magritte, Ed Paschke, Claes Oldenburg, Andy Warhol, Max Ernst and Christo are on display in the nine halls. Particular emphasis is placed on depicting experimental art in various spheres, including painting, photography, video, dance, music and performance. A few artists are interestingly represented in retrospect. From the *M Café* you can look down on some modern statues in a garden. *Open Tue, Thu, Fri 11 am–6 pm, Wed 11 am–9 pm, Sat, Sun 10 am–6 pm, admission US$ 6.50, free on the first Tue in the month, 220 E. Chicago Av., Magnificent Mile, buses 3, 10, 11, 66, 125, 145, 146, 151, subway Red Line to Chicago Street*

Museum of Science and Industry (O)
☛ see map on page 24

★ A world-famous institution in Chicago since 1933 and a model for all other interactive museums in the world. The Museum of Science and Industry should be right at the top of the list of city attractions you intend to visit. The initial impression will astonish you: the magnificent classical edifice was the "Palace of Fine Arts" during the 1893 World Exhibition. You should allow at least three hours for the 2000 and more exhibitions and presentations. On no account should you fail to see the attractions highlighted by coloured pictograms on the official plan. The faithfully reproduced coal-mine, down which visitors can travel in a mine cage, has become one of the best known. Other highlights include walking through a German Second World War U-boat (in an interactive game you have to recognise enemy ships and destroy them) and a partially dismantled Boeing 727, the cockpit of which is open, a breeding station for chicks (you can see the chicks emerging from the egg), a human heart in which you can move freely about, Apollo and Mercury space capsules together with moon rock brought back by the Apollo 17 mission, a main street around the end of the 19th century (together with the noise of horses hooves) and an Idea Factory for computer kids who are introduced to the secrets of science by means of games. In the Omnimax Theater you can see prize-winning documentaries such as "Amazons" in superformat. *Open daily 9.30 am–5.30 pm, admission US$ 7, US$ 12 with Omnimax, free on Thu, 57th St. & Lakeshore Dr., Hyde Park, bus 10 to Museum of Science and Industry*

Polish Museum of America   (O)

This, the oldest museum of an immigrant group, is also the best. Since the 19th century it has provided information on the history and culture of the Polish people and of Polish immigrants to America. Temporary exhibitions also give details of little known Polish artists and the part played by Poles in the Second World War. Special attention is given to the best known Pole, Pope John Paul II. The museum arranges cultural evenings with films, readings and lectures. *Open daily 11 am–4 pm, admission free, 984 N. Milwaukee Av., West Side, subway Blue Line to Division*

Spertus Museum   (111/D 3)

Jewish history focussed through art and culture. The impressive display of over 10,000 exhibits and objets d'art spans 5,000 years of Jewish history. In the Artifact Center young visitors can search for fragments of pottery in a reproduced excavation site. *Open Sun–Thu 10 am–5 pm, Fri 10 am–3 pm, admission US $ 4, 618 S. Michigan Av., Near South, buses 3, 4, 6, 145, 151, 157, subway/El Red to Jackson and Brown, Purple, Orange or Green to Adams Street*

Terra Museum of American Art   (109/D 2)

The art collection of the millionaire Daniel J. Terra is housed in this plain building. The paintings date from the 18th, 19th and 20th centuries. Art lovers enthuse about the unknown artists who can be discovered in this museum. *Open Wed–Sat 10 am–6 pm, Tue 10 am–8 pm, Sun midday–5 pm, admission US$ 5, free on Tue and the first Sun in the month, 666 N. Michigan Av., Magnificent Mile, buses 3, 11, 125, 145, 147, 151, subway Red Line to Chicago Street*

Ukrainian National Museum   (O)

The museum lies in the Ukrainian Village, the hub of Ukrainian immigrants, and provides information about the culture and folklore of this minority race in Chicago. Arts and crafts such as painted eggs, embroidered tablecloths and wood carvings as well as a selection of original costumes demonstrate the skills of the Ukrainian craftsmen and artists. *Open Thu–Sun 11 am–4 pm, admission US$ 2, 721 N. Oakley Bd., West Side, bus 66 to Oakley Boulevard*

Where to dine

The pan pizza was invented and the hot dog refined in Chicago, but discriminating gourmets will also find much to tickle their palates

Al Capone liked his steak well done. In his day Chicago was already known for its first class steakhouses, and even the gangster king sometimes tired of his favourite pasta dishes. After all, most of the cattle in the USA were slaughtered in Chicago and naturally the butchers kept the best meat for themselves. It was similar in the case of pork, but a lot of Americans do not like pork and the pigs are today mostly processed into *frankfurters* and *wiener sausages*. They also go to make hot dogs, the famous American sausage without which no baseball game on the Wrigley Field would be complete and which are sold on every street corner in New York. But they are not real hot dogs, they will tell you in Chicago, because sticking the hot sausage between two halves of a bread roll and covering it with mustard or pickled cabbage is not done. In Chicago the making of a hot dog has been raised to a fine art. The

classic is refined by the addition of aromatic mustard, sweet relish, chopped onions, slices of tomato, celery salt and paprika. And they are just the basics. Every hot dog stand has its own recipe.

The famous pan pizza, too, was invented in Chicago, but not by Pizza Hut. The preparation of the crispy crust is left to the Italians and New Yorkers. A pizza marked *made in Chicago* must lie heavy in the hand and be properly covered. You must have a sharp knife to slice it with.The same goes for the famous steaks and spare ribs. Chicago is an honest city and the people enjoy good plain food. However, that does not mean that gourmets miss out in Chicago. Quite the contrary. The wide ethnic range has resulted in an equally wide spectrum of select restaurants which could compete with the best in Italy, Greece, China or Russia. A whole range of three-star chefs prepare brilliantly innovative dishes and prizewinning cuisine in such world-famous restaurants as the "Everest" or 'Charlie Trotters". Gourmets even fly to the Windy City from New York.

It is not just basketball players who can enjoy good plain cooking at Michael Jordan's

If you wish to visit one of the more popular restaurants in Chicago you will need to book a table. Only in some gourmet restaurants do gentlemen have to wear a jacket and tie. In most American establishments you are shown to your table so that commission is equally shared between all the staff. For lunch most people make do with a sandwich or salad, saving the main meal until the evening, when it is taken comparatively early, usually about 7 pm. Beer with the meal is the exception, people usually order a coffee as they used to do in the old West. But those who miss their European food are also well catered for in Chicago; "The Berghoff" is the best German restaurant in America.

Ben & Jerry's   (107/D 3)

✝ The only branch in Chicago of this legendary ice-cream chain which was started by two men with a sweet tooth in a garage in New England. Here you will find flavours you have always longed for, such as *Cherry Garcia* with cheries and raisins, and *Chocolate Chip Cookie Dough* with pieces of raw cookies and chocolate chips. *338 W. Armitage Av., Lincoln Park, bus 73, El Brown to Sedgewick*

Café Avanti   (O)

An inviting street café, ideal for a cappuccino after a visit to the theatre. Or you could indulge in a *turtle*, an espresso tasting of caramel. There are cakes too. *Open daily 7 am–11 pm, 3706 N.*

MARCO POLO SELECTION: RESTAURANTS

1 Crofton on Wells
American cuisine with vegetables and fine fruits (page 43)

2 Gene and Georgetti's
An institution in the city for 50 years (page 43)

3 The Berghoff
Pickled meat and pork cutlets: German immigrants' cuisine (page 44)

4 Le Colonial
High-class Vietnamese cuisine in a fitting environment (page 44)

5 Spiaggia
Fresh salads and tasty and imaginative pasta dishes (page 46)

6 Tizi Melloul
Franco-Moroccan dishes – something different (page 46)

7 Pizzeria Uno
This is where the pan pizza first saw the light of day (page 51)

8 Bubba Gump Shrimp Company
Peel shrimps like Forrest Gump did (page 47)

9 Blackhawk Lodge
American home cooking just like mum's (page 44)

10 Carson's
The best spare ribs in the city (page 44)

Fancy a "Cherry Garcia"?

Southport Av., North Side, El Brown to Southport

Corner Bakery (108/C 3)

❖ Fantastic sweetmeats and tasty sandwiches in this bakery on the corner. Chicago housewives come from miles away for the bread. Ideal for a budget breakfast. *Open Mon–Fri 6.30 am–9 pm, Sat, Sun 7 am–9 pm, 516 N. Clark St., River North, subway Red Line to Grand/State*

Gourmand Coffeehouse (110/C 2)

This café is said to offer the best cappuccino in Chicago. Even experienced coffee drinkers from Europe will enjoy a visit here. Delicious desserts. *728 Dearborn St., Printers Row, Tel. 312/427 26 10, buses 22, 62, subway Red Line to Harrison*

Margie's Candie (O)

Dates from the 1950s: an ice-cream parlour and soda fountain with atmosphere. Sundaes, shakes and other calorie-rich delights. *Open daily 10 am–11 pm, 1960 N. Western Av., North Side, subway Blue Line to Western Avenue*

Toast (106/B 2)

❖ All-day breakfast: Toast serves all kinds of toast and delicious pancakes. This is just the place for a banana-pecan or mango pancake. Also sandwiches. *Open Tue–Fri 7 am–3 pm, Sat, Sun 8 am–4 pm, 746 W. Webster St., Lincoln Park, Tel. 773/935 56 00, subway Red Line to Fullerton*

RESTAURANTS

Category 1: main course from 20 dollars including drinks

Arun's (O)

Arun Sampanthavivat prepares Thai dishes to perfection. Restaurant critics enthusiastically proclaim it the best Thai restaurant in North America. The dishes are also a visual delight. Definitely order ... la carte (a little bit of everything)! *Open Tue–Sat 5–10 pm, Sun 5–9.30 pm, 4156 N. Kedzie Av., North Side, Tel. 773/539-1909, bus 90 to Irving Park Road*

Bice (109/D 2)

Founded in 1926 by an immigrant from Milan and for some years now a renowned name in both Chicago and Beverley Hills. Northern Italian dishes are served on several floors, the pasta being especially recommended. *Open Mon–Thu 11.30 am–10.30 pm, Fri–Sat 11.30 am–11 pm, 158 E. Ontario St., Near North, Tel. 312/664 14 74, subway Red Line to Grand/State*

Gourmet Restaurants in Chicago

Ambria (O)

Intimate ambience and attentive service in one of the best restaurants in the USA. Chef Gabino Sotelino serves Gallic cordon bleu dishes to perfection. Booked up weeks in advance! *Open Mon–Thu 6–9.30 pm, Fri, Sat 6–10.30 pm, 2300 Lincoln Park West, Lincoln Park, Tel. 773/472 00 76, bus 151*

Charlie Trotters (106/B 3)

Frequently elected the best restaurant in Chicago. The menu changes daily and ranges from antelope steak to ravioli with shitake mushrooms. Nouvelle cuisine as it has never been cooked before. The Californian wines are certainly not to be despised. If possible reserve a table weeks in advance! *Open Tue–Sat 5.30–11 pm, 816 W. Armitage Av., Lincoln Park, Tel. 773/248 62 28, El Brown to Armitage*

Everest (110/B 2)

Alsatian gourmet cuisine in the elite LaSalle Club on the 40th floor high above the roofs of Chicago. Chef Jean Joho, who began his career as a baker's apprentice in Strasbourg, magics up first-class dishes from fresh seafood and tender veal. To date the city's most innovative cuisine. *Open Tue–Thu 5.30–9 pm, Fri, Sat 5.30–10 pm, 440 S. LaSalle St., in the Loop, Tel. 312/663 89 20, El Brown to LaSalle/Van Buren*

Nick's Fishmarket Restaurant (108/B 2)

Fresh fish from the Pacific, flown in daily from Hawaii, is one of the specialities of this modern gourmet temple located in front of the Chagall Mosaic in the Loop. Beautiful surroundings, good service, the best food. *Open Mon–Thu 11.30 am–3 pm and 5.30–11.30 pm, Fri 11.30 am–3 pm and 5.30 pm–midnight, Sat 5.30pm–midnight, First National Bank Plaza, in the Loop, Tel. 312/612 02 00, subway Red, Blue Lines to Monroe*

Le Français (O)

Number one in the view of most restaurant critics, spoiled slightly by the somewhat boring atmosphere. Roland Liccioni serves completely French epicure dishes. Absolutely perfect service. *Open Tue–Fri 11.30 am–2 pm, Mon–Sat 5.30–9 pm, 269 S. Milwaukee Av., North Side, Wheeling, Tel. 847/541 74 70, bus 56*

Shaw's Crab House and Blue Crab Lounge (109/D 3)

Actually two restaurants with first-class seafood. In the Crab House you can dine on superb salmon in a fine mustard sauce, while in the (cheaper) Blue Crab Lounge you can order the city's best Crab Cake and best oysters. *Open daily 11.30 am–2 pm and 5–11 pm, 21 E. Hubbard St., Near North, Tel. 312/527 27 22, subway Red Line to Grand/State*

Biggs Restaurant (107/E 5)

Fine American cuisine in a magnificent 1930s building. Al Capone and his upper-class friends could well have dined here. A supper club atmosphere with light and elegant paintwork. *Open Sun–Thu 5–10 pm, Fri and Sat 5–11 pm, 1150 N. Dearborn St., Near North, Tel. 312/787 09 00, subway Red Line to Clark/Division*

Cape Cod Room (109/D 1)

Little has changed since the 1950s in this elegant seafood restaurant – neither the dusty but elegant ambience nor the extremely attentive staff. The fine fish from Atlantic waters tastes as delicious as its has always done. *Open daily midday–11.30 pm, 140 E. Walton Place (in the Drake Hotel), Magnificent Mile, Tel. 312/787 22 00, subway Red Line to Chicago/State*

Coco Pazzo (108/B 2)

Excellent home cooking from Tuscany, perhaps the best Italian restaurant in the city. The original is in New York. Even risottos and pizzas are not prepared better in Italy itself. *Open daily 11.30 am–2.30 pm, Mon–Thu 5.15–10.30 pm, Fri, Sat 5.15–11 pm, 300 W. Hubbard St., River North, Tel. 312/836 09 00, El Brown to Merchandise Mart*

Crofton on Wells (108/C 3)

★ ☯ Suzy Crofton is one of the best-known and best lady chefs in Chicago. In her little restaurant she serves American cuisine with vegetables and fruit. *Open Mon–Thu 11.30–2.30 pm and 5.30–10 pm, Fri 11.30 am–2.30 pm and 5.30–11 pm, Sat 5.30–11 pm, 535 N. Wells St., River North, Tel.* 312/755 17 90, El Brown to Merchandise Mart

Gene and Georgetti's (108/B 3)

★ Said to be the best steakhouse in the city, an institution for more than 50 years. The first-class meals are a bit pricy. *Open Mon–Sat 11 am–midnight, 500 N. Franklin St., River North, Tel. 312/527 37 18, El Brown to Merchandise Mart*

Gibson's Steakhouse (107/E 6)

Most guests come for the succulent steaks, but some come just to spot a prominent figure or to be seen themselves. Even more renowned than the steaks are the giant Martinis! *Open Mon–Sat 5–midnight, Sun 5–midnight, 1028 N. Rush St., Near North, Tel. 312/266 89 99, subway Red Line to Clark/Division*

Hatsuhana (109/D 2)

A first-class sushi bar with a sober Japanese ambience. The fish is superfresh! *Open Mon–Fri 11.45 am–2 pm and 5.30–10 pm, Sat 5–10 pm, 160 E. Ontario St., Magnificent Mile, Tel. 312/280 88 08, subway Red Line to Grand/State*

Pump Room (107/E 5)

Among the (often very good) hotel restaurants in Chicago this is one of the best. Classical American cuisine with a French touch. The atmosphere has remained conservative following renovation and men must wear jackets. *Open daily 11.30 am–2.30 pm, also Mon–Thu 6–10 pm, Fri, Sat 5 pm–midnight, Sun 5 pm–midnight, 1301 N. State Parkwa (in the Omni Ambassador), Near North, Tel. 312/266 0360, subway Red Line to Clark/Division*

Rosebud on Rush (109/D 2)

The portions are so large that "you will not be hungry again for three years", as one restaurant critic put it. The portions are truly gigantic, and the Chicken Vesuvio tastes wonderful. *Open Mon–Thu 10 am–3 pm, 5–10.30 pm, Fri 10 am–3 pm, 5–11.30 pm, Sat 11 am–3 pm, 5–11 pm, Sun midday–3 pm, 4–9.30 pm, 720 N. Rush St., Near North, Tel. 312/266 64 44, subway Red Line to Chicago/State*

The Saloon (109/D 1)

This elegant steakhouse has little in common with saloons. The atmosphere here is in fact peaceful and unobtrusive. The steaks melt on the tongue, but are expensive here compared with other restaurants. *Open Mon–Thu 11.30 am–10.30 pm, Fri, Sat 11.30 am–11 pm, Sun midday–10 pm, 200 E. Chestnut St., Near North, Tel. 312/280 54 54, subway Red Line to Chicago/State.*

Category 2: main course between 15 and 20 dollars including drinks

The Berghoff (109/D 5)

★ ✪ Founded in 1898 by a German immigrant and since then a classic among Chicago restaurants. German cuisine which will suit German visitors. *Open Mon–Thu 11 am–9 pm, Fri 11 am–9.30 pm, Sat 11 am–10 pm, 17 W. Adams St., in the Loop, Tel. 312/427 31 70, El Green, Brown, Purple, Orange to Adams Street*

Blackhawk Lodge (109/D 2)

★ Fine American home cooking in rustic surroundings. The portions (e.g. roast chicken with mashed potato and vegetables) are extremely large. *Open Mon–Thu 11 am–3 pm and 5–10 pm, Fri, Sat 11 am–3 pm and 5–11 pm, Sun 11 am–3 pm and 5–10 pm, 41 E. Superior St., Near North, Tel. 312/280 40 80, subway Red Line to Chicago/State*

Bluepoint Oyster Bar (108/A 4)

Well-kept 40 year-old chic establishment. They serve fresh oysters and a selection of innovative fish dishes. *Open Mon–Thu 11 am–10 pm, Fri 11.30 am–midnight, Sun 5–9.30 pm, 741 W. Randolph St, west of the Loop, Tel. 312/207 12 22, El Brown, Green, Orange, Purple to Lake*

Carson's (108/C 2)

★ "The place for ribs" it states above the entrance, and that says it all. Here you can get the best spare ribs in Chicago. *Open Mon–Thu 11 am–11 pm, Fri 11 am–12.30 am, Sat midday–11 pm, Sun midday–1 pm, 612 N. Wells, River North, Tel. 312/280 92 00, subway Red Line to Grand/State*

Centro (108/C 2)

Yuppy restaurant and haunt of show-offs, but the food is good: finest North Italian cuisine with tasty salads and good pasta. *Open Mon–Thu 11 am–11 pm, Fri 11 am–11.30 pm, Sat midday –11.30 pm, Sun 4–10 pm, 710 N. Wells St., River North, Tel. 312/988 77 75, El Brown to Chicago Street*

Le Colonial (109/D 1)

★ Old Saigon in a pleasant townhouse with a terrace. The palm trees and rattan furniture fit the name and the Vietnamese menu. The exotically spiced fish is specially recommended. *Open Mon–Sat midday–2.30 pm, also Mon–Fri 5–11 pm, Sat 5 pm–mid-*

night, Sun 5–10 pm, 937 N. Rush St., Near North, Tel. 312/255 00 88, subway Red to ChicagoState

Michael Jordan's (108/C 3)

♱ Restaurant owned by the basketball legend Michael Jordan. However, the ex-star of the Chicago Bulls is seldom seen here. The plain American fare tastes astonishly good. *Open Sun–Thu 11.30 am–10.30 pm, Fri, Sat 11.30 am–midnight, 500 N. LaSalle St., River North, Tel. 312/644-DUNK, El Brown to Merchandise Mart*

Pasteur (O)

South-east Asia in a pleasant and cosy establishment with rattan furniture. A full range of Vietnamese dishes, the best being the fish. *Open Mon, Tue 5–10 pm, Wed, Thu, Sun midday–10 pm, Fri, Sat midday–11 pm, 5525 N. Broadway, North Side, Tel. 773/878 10 61, bus 36, subway Red Line to Bryn Mawr*

Restaurant Okno (O)

High-tech ambience in a futuristic restaurant, The designer was inspired by the cult film "A Clockwork Orange". An innovative mix of Western and South American cuisine. *Open Sun–Thu 5.30–11.30 pm, Fri, Sat 5.30 pm–12.30 am, 1332 N. Milwaukee Av., Wicker Park, Tel. 773/395 13 13, subway Blue Line to Division*

Russian Tea Time (109/D 5)

Dark but cosy. Regular haunt of many operagoers. A full range of Russian dishes; for those new to it we recommend the plate of mixed hors d'oeuvres. *Open Sun, Mon 11 am–9 pm, Tue–Thu 11 am–11 pm, Fri, Sat 11 am–midnight, 77 E. Adams St., in the Loop, Tel. 312/360 00 00, El Brown, Green, Orange, Purple to Adams St.*

Lunchtime by the Chicago River with a view of the skyscrapers

Signature Room at the 95th (109/D 1)

American kitchen high above the roofs of Chicago, on the 95th floor of the John Hancock Center. The view is breathtaking and the Sunday brunch with live jazz music is an extra pleasure. *Brunch Sun 10.30 am–2.30 pm, lunch Mon–Sat 11 am–2.30 pm, dinner Sun–Thu 5–11 pm, Fri, Sat 5–11.30 pm, 875 N. Michigan Av., Magnificent Mile, Tel. 312/787 95 96, buses 125, 145, 146, 147, 151, subway Red Line to Chicago/State*

Spago (108/C 3)

Beverly Hills is not enough for him; the famous chef Wolfgang Puck is now working his magic in Chicago too. His Pacific-Rim cuisine combines Asiatic and Californian cooking. *Open Mon–Thu 11.30 am–1 pm and 5–9.30 pm, Fri 11.30 am–1 pm and 5–10.30 pm, Sat 5–10.30 pm, Sun 5–9.30 pm, 520 N. Dearham St., River North, Tel. 312/527 37 00, subway Red Line to Grand/State*

Spiaggia (109/D 1)

★ First class salads and pasta using superfresh ingredients served in avant-garde surroundings. A view over Lake Michigan is included in the price. *Open Mon–Thu 11.30 am–2 pm and 5.30–9 pm, Fri, Sat 11.30 am–2 pm and 5.30–10 pm, Sun 11.30 am–9 pm, 980 N. Michigan Av., Magnificent Mile, Tel. 312/280 27 50, subway Red Line to Chicago/State*

Las Tablas (O)

A pleasant street restaurant in Lincoln Park. South American feel and tasty dishes from Colombia, e.g. New York Steak with fried yucca. *Open Mon–Thu midday–10 pm, Fri, Sat midday–11 pm, 2965 N. Lincoln Av., Lincoln Park, Tel. 773/871 24 14, El Brown to Diversy*

Tizi Melloul (108/C 3)

★ Moroccan dishes with a French touch in a very dark restaurant with Arab overtones. Very fine cuisine, e.g. duck in a ginger sauce with wild rice and raisins. *Open daily 11.30 am–2 pm and 5–10 pm, 531 N. Wells St., River North, Tel. 312/670 43 38, El Brown to Merchandise Mart*

Toque (108/A 4)

Original French cuisine (e.g. halibut wrapped in bacon with a puree of sweet peas and cocktail onions) in bright and friendly surroundings. *Open Mon–Fri 11.30 am–11.30 pm, Sat 5–11.30 pm, Sun 5–10 pm, 816 W. Randolph St., west of the Loop, Tel. 312/666 11 00, El Brown, Green, Orange, Purple to Lake*

Trattoria No. 10 (108/C 4)

Cheerful colours from Tuscany surround you in this classic Italian restaurant. Its specialities include fantastic ravioli dishes. *Open Mon–Thu 11.30 am–2 pm and 5.30–9 pm, Fri 11.30 am–2 pm and 5.30–10 pm, Sat 5.30–10 pm, 10 N. Dearborn St., in the Loop, Tel. 312/984 17 18, subway Blue Line to Washington*

160blue (O)

The unusual name refers to the house number and the blue colour in which it is painted, but it is somewhat avant-garde inside too, being the work of a top interior decorator, while in the kitchen star chef Patrick Robertson conjures up some unusual dishes such as lamb T-bone steak with Japanese artichokes. *Open Mon–Thu 5–10 pm, Fri, Sat 5–11 pm, 160 N. Loomis St., west of the Loop, Tel. 312/850 03 03, El Brown, Green, Orange, Purple to Lake*

Category 3: main course between 7 and 15 dollars including drinks

Ann Sather (O)
❂ A Swedish immigrant establishment with cult status. A bold mix of American and Scandinavian cooking which goes down well in the neighbourhood. The Swedish meat dumplings also have a Mediterranean taste. *Open Sun–Thu 7 pm–10 pm, Fri, Sat 7 am–11 pm, 929 Belmont Av., North Side, Tel. 773/348 23 78, subway Red Line to Belmont*

Billy Goat Tavern (109/D 3)
A journalists' pub just like you see in films: loud, rather uncomfortable but full of atmosphere. There is football on the television, greasy cheeseburgers on the table, thin beer at the bar. *Open Mon–Sat 7 am–2 am, Sun 11 am–2 am, 430 N. Michigan Av., Magnificent Mile, Tel. 312/22 215 25, El Brown Green, Purple, Orange to State Street*

Brasserie Jo (108/C 3)
Cheap subsidiary of the high-class Everest restaurant the 40 year-old interior of which (lush plants and plenty of light) and smartly dressed waiters remind you of that patronised by the gangsters in the film. Only Al Capone never thought about Alsace cuisine. *Open Mon–Thu 11.30 am–4 pm and 5–10 pm, Fri 11.30 am–4 pm and 5–11 pm, Sun 5–10 pm, 59 W. Hubbard, River North, Tel. 312/595 08 00, subway/El Red to Grand/State and Brown to Merchandise Mart*

Bubba Gump Shrimp Company (109/D 3)
★ In the cult film of the same name the protagonist Forrest Gump (among others) was a successful shrimp fisherman. As well as shrimps, fish and chips and BBQ ribs are served in this idyllic restaurant. *Open Sun–Thu 11 am–11 pm, Fri, Sat 11 am–midnight, 700 E. Grand Av. (Navy Pier), east of the Loop, Tel. 312/595 55 00, buses 29, 56, 65, 66, 120, 121 to Navy Pier*

Café Iberico (108/C 2)
South American *tapas* are served on two floors under a "sky" of tiles and wine bottles. Speciality dishes include grilled octopus and grilled salmon with green peppers. *Open Mon–Thu 11 am–11 pm, Fri 11 am–1.30 am, Sat midday–1.30 am, Sun midday–11 pm, 739 LaSalle St., Lincoln Park, Tel. 312/573 15 10, subway/El Red to Chicago/State St. and Brown to Chicago Street*

Edwardo's (107/E 5)
Specialises in juicy pan pizzas done as people like them in Chicago. Those with a big appetite will get value for money with the All You Can Eat Pizza. *Open Sun–Thu 11 am–11 pm, Fri, Sat 11 am–midnight, 1212 N. Dearborn St., River North, Tel. 312/337 44 90, subway Red Line to Clarke/Division*

Goose Island Brewing Company (106/B 4)
Microbreweries have been all the rage in the USA for some time

now. The home-brewed beer does not taste any better but the atmosphere is okay and the potato crisps are free! *Open Mon–Thu 11 am–midnight, Fri, Sat 11 am–2 am, Sun 11 am–11 pm, 1800 N. Clybourn Av., Lincoln Park, Tel. 312/915 00 71, subway Red Line to North Av./Clybourn*

Green Door Tavern (108/B 2)
Since 1921 an institution in a crooked wooden building. There are American sandwiches, and the hickory burger would satisfy even a grown-up cowboy. *Open Mon–Thu 11 am–11 pm, Fri 11 am–1.30 pm, Sat midday–1.30 am, Sun midday–11 pm, 730 LaSalle St., River North, Tel. 312/664 54 96, subway/El Red to Chicago/State, Brown to Chicago St.*

Harry Caray's (108/C 3)
Harry Caray was a famous baseball reporter who retired and opened this restaurant. Surrounded by baseball souvenirs you can enjoy good solid American fare. *Open Mon–Thu 11.30–3 pm and 5–10.30 pm, Fri 11.30 am–3 pm, 5–11 pm, Sat 11.30 am–4 pm and 5–11 pm, Sun midday–10 pm, 33 W. Kinzie St., River North, Tel. 312/828 09 66, subway/El Brown to Merchandise Mart and Red to Grand/State, Category 3*

Mambo Grill (108/C 3)
Fantastic *tapas* from Mexico, Cuba and South America in a spacious and bright restaurant in River North. The black beans are particularly good – and the flan!

Harry Caray's: enjoy good substantial meals surrounded by baseball mementos

Open Mon–Thu 11 am–10 pm, Fri
11 am–11 pm, Sat midday–11 pm,
Sun 5–9 pm, 412 N. Clark St., River
North, Tel. 312/467 97 97, El
Brown to Merchandise Mart

Mitty Nice Grill (109/D 1)

Small, relatively cheap place in
the Water Tower Place Shopping
Mall. The meat loaf with mashed
potatoes and green beans tastes
best and costs less than ten dollars. Open Mon–Sat 11 am–10 pm,
Sun 11 am–9 pm, 835 N. Michigan
Av., Magnificent Mile, Tel. 312/335
47 45, subway Red Line to Chicago
Street

Mrs Levy's (108/B 5)

Jewish delicatessen with reasonable bagels together with
salmon and cream cheese,
potato pancakes and other
snacks. Open Mon–Fri 6.30 am–3
am, 233 S. Wacker Dr., (in Sears
Tower), near the Loop, Tel.
312/993 05 30, El Brown, Orange
to Quincy

Northside Tavern (O)

Basic establishment with a particularly pretty inner courtyard in
the trendy new quarter of
Wicker Park. The burgers are
good and cheap, for lunch there
are tasty specials like chicken
salad. Open Sun–Fri 11.30 am–2
am, Sat 11 am–3 am, 1635 N.
Damen Av., Wicker Park, Tel.
773/384 35 55, subway Blue Line
to Damen

The Potbelly Sandwich (O)

✪ ✗ Ambience less than nil, but
the sandwiches are among the
best in town. The college kids,
who are among the regular
patrons, favour ham and cheese.
Open daily 11 am–2 pm and 5–10

pm, 2264 N. Lincoln Av., North
Side, bus 11

Scoozi (108/B 2)

Classical music and free pizza
while waiting to be shown to
your table, but the wait is worthwhile, The noodles would not
taste any better in Italy, and the
gnocchi with tomato sauce are a
dream! Open Mon–Thu 11.30
am–2 pm and 5–9.30 pm, Fri 11.30
am–2 pm and 5–10.30 pm, Sat
5–10.30 pm, Sun 4–9 pm, 410 W.
Huron St., River North, Tel.
312/943 59 00, subway Red Line to
Chicago Street

Soprafina Marketcaffé, (108/C 4)

The pizzas and bread taste surprisingly Italian, namely crisp
and crusty, and you can see what
the fillings look like. Do not be
put off by the fact that it is self-
service. Open Mon–Fri 11 am–4
pm, 10 N. Dearborn St.,in the Loop,
subway Red Line to Monroe/State

Three Happiness (112/B 2)

❋ Looks a nasty low dive, but is
in fact one of the best and most
authentic Chinese restaurants in
town. Plain cooking from the
China of old, prepared and
served by the family, Open daily 9
am–2 pm, 209 Cermak Rd., Chinatown, Tel. 312/842 19 64, subway
Red Line to Chinatown

Wishbone (O)

Excellent plain fare for the dis-
cerning "lunch crowd" with
unusual dishes such as "Hoppin'
Jack" (peas and beans on brown
rice garnished with cheese,
onions and tomatoes). Oprah
Winfey has been seen in here
before now. Open Mon 7 am–3
pm, Tue–Thu 7 am–10 pm, Fri 7

am–11 pm, Sat 8 am–11 pm, Sun 8 am–2.30 pm, 1001 W. Washington St., west of the Loop, Tel. 312/850 26 63, buses 8, 9

Yoshi's Café (O)
A happy mix of Japanese and French cuisine, the fruits of the sea and the fish taste the best. Try the shrimp tempura! The atmosphere is a bit boring. *Open Tue–Thu 5–10.30 pm, Fri, Sat 5–11 pm, Sun 5–9.30 pm, 3257 N. Halsted St., North Side, Tel. 773/248 61 60, subway Red Line to Belmomt*

Fast food

Fluky's (O)
Hot-dog fans swear by this classic establishment which serves "singles" or "doubles" with mustard, onions, relish, gurkins and tomatoes. *Open daily 7 am–10 pm, 6821 N. Western Av., North Side, Tel. 773/274 36 52, subway Blue Line to Western Avenue*

Foodlife (109/D 1)
A flamboyant street of snack bars with some smart places serving healthy and low-calorie salads as well as exotic delicacies. You can dine under artificial trees in Water Tower Place. *Open Sun–Thu 7.30 am–9 pm, Fri, Sat 11 am–10 pm, 835 N. Michigan Av., Magnificent Mile, Tel. 312/335 36 63, subway Red Line to Chicago Street*

Gold Coast Dogs (109/D 3)
Try the genuine hot dogs just as they were invented in Chicago. Do not forget the relish and paprika! *Open Mon–Fri 7 am–10 pm, Sat, Sun 11 am–8 pm, 418 State St., north of the Loop, El Brown, Green, Orange, Purple to State Street*

Jim's Hot Dog Stand (108/A 6)
A lot of policemen eat here, so that is like a seal of approval. The hot dogs and spicy Polish sausages are among the best that Chicago fast food outlets can

Memories of the 1950s in Rock 'n' Roll McDonald's

offer. *Open 24 hours, 1320 S, Halsted St., south of the Loop, Tel. 312/666 05 33, subway Blue Line to Halsted*

Pizzeria Uno (109/D 3)
★ The famous pan pizza was invented in this narrow shed, and nobody in Chicago ever mentions the name Pizza Hut. *Open Mon–Fri 11.30 am–1 am, Sat 11.30 am–2 am, Sun 11.30 am–11 pm, 29 East Ohio St., River North, Tel. 312/321 10 00, subway Red Line to Grand*

Theme restaurants

ESPN Zone (109/D 3)
ESPN is the best known sports channel in the USA. Sports fans enjoy their steaks in a TV studio surrounded by flickering screens showing football, baseball and basketball matches. Only for those keen on sport! *Open daily 11 am–11 pm, 41 E. Ohio St., River North, Tel. 312/644 37 76, subway Red Line to Grand/State, Category 3*

House of Blues (108/C 3)
You can enjoy good honest Southern States cooking from the Mississippi delta while at the same time looking at portraits of well-known blues legends, to the sound of music from aspiring blues players. *Open daily 11.30 am–midnight, 329 N. Dearborn St., River North, Tel. 312/923 20 07, subway/El Red to Grand/State, Brown to Merchandise Mart, Category 3*

Rainforest Café (108/C 3)
☘ Invisible apes roar in an arti-

Tarzan sends his regards: young people meet in the Rainforest Café

ficial rainforest, accompanied by a rushing waterfall. Chicago has its new theme restaurants too. The sandwiches are just an extra. *Open Mon–Thu, Sun 11 am–11 pm, Fri, Sat 11.30 am–midnight, 605 N. Clark St., River North, Tel. 312/787 15 01, subway Red Line to Grand/State, Category 3*

Rock 'n' Roll McDonald's (108/C 2–3)
☘ McDonald's goes Hard Rock Café (the usual one is opposite). Kitsch memorabilia from the rock 'n' roll era from stars such as Elvis to the Beatles surround the customer as he eats his Big Mac or McNuggets. *Open Sun–Thu 6 am–3 am, Fri, Sat 6 am–5 am, 600 N. Clark St., River North, Tel. 312/664 79 40, subway Red Line to Grand/State, Category 3*

Shopping with style

Shopping is a Chicago tradition, and it is a pleasure in such attractive shopping areas as the Magnificent Mile

Trading was done in Chicago back in the pioneering days. Cattle and pigs from the West were brought into the abattoirs and their meat, fresh or canned, was sold to dealers from the East Coast. The founders of the large mail order firms such as Sears and Montgomery came from the Windy City. The multi-storeyed Merchandise Mart, already an institution many decades ago, still exists today, and Marshall Field's, the store owned by a prosperous citizen, maintains it position in the face of competition from New York.

Chicago has moved with the times, follows all the trends which originate in New York City or Los Angeles, and is a second home to successful chains such as Borders Books, Virgin Music and Toys 'R Us. The most stylish shopping street and the one most popular with tourists is the *Mag Mile*. as the locals call their Magnificent Mile, North Michigan Avenue between Oak Street and Chicago River. Even Tiffanys and Saks Fifth Avenue

are established here. Nobody in Chicago will accept comparisons with Rodeo Drive in Beverly Hills or Fifth Avenue in New York, because the Mag Mile is far more impressive. And just as expensive. Little shops, original galleries and hip boutiques have set up in the trendy new quarters like River North and Wicker Park. There you will even find fashion-conscious punks. Souvenirs can be bought on Navy Pier or in the Tribune Store. Considerably cheaper are the goods in the Loop and State Street, the main shopping thoroughfare under the elevated railway.

Unless indicated otherwise, shops are open daily during the week from 10 am–6 or 7 pm and on Sundays from 10 am or midday to 5 or 6 pm. In the Loop they are closed on Sundays. When checking prices always remember there is a value added tax of 8.75 per cent. Cheaper than in most European countries are propri-etary brands of jeans, cosmetics and designer clothing – but only if the dollar does not go up! Anyone flying to the West of America should buy their jeans there, where you will save even more.

Michigan Avenue, the "Magnificent Mile" shopping street

MARCO POLO SELECTION: SHOPPING

1 The Chicago Architecture Foundation Gift Shop
Everything to do with the legendary skyscrapers (page 54)

2 Borders Books & Music
Books, books, books – all the magazines (page 55)

3 900 North Michigan Shops
Smart shops all under one roof (page 58)

4 Marshall Field's
Treat the department store king with due reverence (page 57)

5 Eddie Bauer
Trendy gear with a sporty note (page 56)

6 Virgin Megastore
The world's largest record store! (page 57)

7 Accent Chicago
The only shop selling genuine souvenirs of the city (page 58)

8 Cookies By Design
Most unusual: cookies with autographs (page 59)

9 NikeTown Chicago
Where trendy buyers go for their sneakers (page 59)

10 Big Chicago Records, Inc.
Chicago blues and jazz on CD – the best souvenir (page 58)

ANTIQUES

Jay Robert's Antique Warehouse (108/C 3)
A whole warehouse full of antiques, from four-poster beds from the colonial period to antique clocks from the end of the 19th century. Important: in the USA junk and kitsch from the 1950s also goes under the heading of antiques. *149 Kinzie St., River North, El Brown, Purple to Merchandise Mart*

Wrigleyville Antique Mall (O)
Collectors' hearts will beat faster here, for in this mall there is everything you could wish from the 1950s. All the items on the two giant floors date from the 20th century and are absolutely charming. For example, there are old advertising boards or cigarette cards of old locomotives or motor cars. *3336 N. Clark St., Wrigleyville, subway Red Line to Clark/Division*

ARCHITECTURE

Chicago Architecture Foundation (109/D 1)
★ After a guided tour of the Chicago Architecture Foundation you can visit the gift shop, but this gift shop sells more than just the usual kitsch. There is a particularly large and varied selection of books on architecture, and there are also ornaments and other souvenirs with architectural motifs of Chicago. *Open daily 9 am–7 pm, 875 N. Michigan Av., Magnificent Mile, subway Red Line to Chicago Street*

SHOPPING

ARTS & CRAFTS

The Alaska Shop Gallery of Eskimo Art (107/E 6)
Soapstone figures, ebony carvings and other craft work of the Inuits, as well as a picture gallery and art from Alaska, Canada and Siberia. *Open Mon–Sat 11 am–5 pm, Near North, 104 E. Oak St., buses 22, 70 to Oak Street*

To Life! (109/D 5)
Everything here is handmade; marionettes, jewellery, puzzles, toys, toy clocks, figures, wonderful work by craftsmen and artists. *224 S. Michigan Av., El (all lines), to Adams Street*

Steve Starr Studios (O)
Tiny shops with a large selection of art deco items from lamps to jewellery. On the walls hang pictures of the great Hollywood stars of the period – in art deco frames, of course. *2779 N. Lincoln Av., east of the Loop, El Brown, Purple to Diversey*

Tobai (108/C 3)
This is the best place for anybody particularly seeking Japanese prints and Korean temple paintings. They also sell paintings by contemporary Chinese artists. *320 N. Dearborn Av., Loop, El Brown, Orange, Green to State/Lake*

BALLOONS

The American Balloon Company (O)
Souvenirs of a special kind: balloons with the logo of an associate's firm, the name of a friend or whatever inscription you wish.

5554 N. Winthrop, subway Red Line to Bryn Mawr

BOOKS

Abraham Lincoln Bookshop (108/B 2)
Only in the land of Abraham Lincoln will you find a bookshop dealing exclusively in books on the legendary president of the Civil War period. You can also buy long-forgotten doctoral theses and letters on the subject. *357 W. Chicago Av., subway Red Line to Chicago Street*

Borders Books & Music (109/D 1)
★ ✪ The USA's best chain of bookshops on the Magnificent Mile. Here you can buy books on any subject at favourable prices and then examine your purchases in the café. *830 N. Michigan Av., Magnificent Mile, subway Red Line to Chicago Street*

BUTTONS

Renaissance Buttons (106/B 3)
Count the buttons? Impossible in this shop, for there are several thousands of them. Antique and modern, gilt and multicoloured, plain and valuable, just about any sort you could possibly imagine on a jacket (or anywhere else). Buttons as a souvenir? This is the place. *826 W. Armitage Av., Lincoln Park, subway Red Line to Armitage*

CIGARS

La Havanita Cigar Factory (109/F 3)
Because nothing may be imported from Cuba the tobacco comes from the Dominican Republic, but it is grown from

Shopping in the Atrium Mall – sheer architectural poetry

Cuban seed. Nimble-fingered Cubans make it into expensive cigars. *600 E. Grand Av., Navy Pier, buses 29, 56, 65, 66, 120, 121 to Navy Pier*

CLOTHING

Banana Republic **(109/D 2)**
This former safari shop has become a normal clothes shop but the choice, especially of light and low-priced gear, still makes it

worth a visit. *Open Mon–Sat 10 am–7 pm, Sun 11 am–6 pm, River North, subway Red Line to Grand Avenue*

Eddie Bauer **(109/D 2)**
★ Together with Tommy Hilfiger, Eddie Bauer is the new cult name in the USA. His products are still hard to obtain in Europe: trendy sports clothes in bright colours and (important) with the famous logo. To make shopping

56

easier there is a coffee bar in the shop. *Open Mon–Sat 10 am–7 pm, Sun 11 am–6 pm, 600 N. Michigan Av., River North, subway Red Line to Grand Avenue*

Timberland (109/D 3)
Robust but trendy footwear and walking shoes are surprisingly cheap in the USA. Ideal for a strenuous tour of the city or walking inland to the Great Lakes. *545 N. Michigan Av., River North, subway Red Line to Grand Avenue*

DEPARTMENT STORE

Marshall Field's (109/D 4)
★ ✿ The king of Chicago department stores sells everything under one roof at astonishingly low prices. It even deals in antiques and antique books. In the confectionery department the firm's own Frango Mints in all colours are especially popular. *111 N. State St., Loop, subway Red Line to Lake Street*

JEWELLERY

Tiffany & Co. (109/D 1)
Almost as big as the original shop in New York and with equally exclusive items. On the ground floor alone there are jewels worth several million dollars. For the smaller purse there are souvenirs for under 100 dollars. Also on sale are expensive gifts in leather, porcelain and crystal as well as watches and cosmetic items all with the famous logo. *Open Mon–Wed 10 am–6 pm, Thu 10 am–7 pm, Fri, Sat 10 am–6 pm, 730 N. Michigan Av., Magnificent Mile, subway Red Line to Chicago Avenue*

MUSIC

The Chicago Music Mart at DePaul Center (109/D 6)
A whole shopping centre selling only musical instruments, music and everything a musician's heart desires. Aspiring musicians even perform in some shops. *333 State St., Loop, subway Red Line to Washington*

Virgin Megastore (109/D 3)
★ ⚡ The world's largest record store has one of its best branches in Chicago. Here are all the CDs, videos, DVDs and cassettes you can imagine, from rock to country music. Older CDs are sold at special prices. *Open Mon–Thu 10 am–11 pm, Fri, Sat 10 am–midnight, Sun 10 am–10 pm, 540 N. Michigan Av., Magnificent Mile, subway Red Line to Chicago Street*

POPCORN

Garrett Popcorn Shop (109/D 2)
Forget the popcorn you buy in European cinemas! Here is the genuine American super-popcorn in all sizes and all colours. The giant bag with its rainbow-coloured crunchy contents also makes a good souvenir. *670 N. Michigan Av., Magnificent Mile, subway Red Line to Grand/State*

SHOPPING CENTRES

The Atrium Mall (108/C 4)
There are many retail shops in the James R. Thompson Center, one of Chicago's most interesting skyscrapers. The unique architectural surroundings are attractive and so are the goods

on display. *Open Mon–Fri 8 am–6 pm, Sat 11 am–4 pm, 100 W. Randolph St., Loop, El (all lines) to Clark Street*

Gurnee Mills Mall (O)
Over 200 factory outlets selling branded goods at rock-bottom prices. Particularly cheap are clothing items with tiny and barely visible flaws. *Open Mon–Sat 10 am–7 pm, Sun midday–5 pm, Interstate 94 and Route 132 West (Grand Av.), North Side, suburban train to Gurnee (about one hour's travelling time)*

Water Tower Place (109/D 1)
Right next to the historic Water Tower this fine mall lies hidden behind a rather ordinary frontage. Over 100 popular shops, a number of

The legendary jewellers Tiffany can be found in Chicago too

restaurants and seven cinemas. *Open Mon–Thu 10 am–7 pm, Fri 10 am–8 pm, Sat 10 am–6 pm, Sun midday–6 pm, 835 N. Michigan Av., Magnificent Mile, subway Red Line to Chicago Street*

900 North Michigan Shops (109/D 1)
★ The best address on the Magnificent Mile with Bloomingdale's and more than 70 well-known shops and designer establishments. Like any mall, there are also cinemas and restaurants. *Open Mon–Thu 10 am–7 pm, Sat 10 am–6 pm, Sun midday–6 pm, 900 N. Michigan Av., Magnificent Mile, subway Red Line to Chicago Street*

SOUVENIRS

Accent Chicago (109/D 2)
★ In this shop everything reflects Chicago – T-shirts, sweatshirts, toys, postcards, mugs, flags, dolls, handkerchiefs, baseball caps and much more – all with the logo of the Windy City. *875 N. Michigan Av., Magnificent Mile, subway Red Line to Chicago Street*

Big Chicago Records, Inc. (O)
★ For all those who wish to listen to the sounds of Chicago and take them home, with them: jazz and blues CDs and the double CD "A Chicago Blues Tour" and "A Chicago Jazz Tour", which is a guided tour of the city's music scene. *909 Forest Av., suburban train (about a one hour journey)*

Chicago Tribune Gift Store (109/D 3)
Souvenirs with the legendary

newspaper's logo are sold in its skyscraper building. An original souvenir for people who like reading newspapers – its title pages are even printed on T-shirts and sweat-shirts. *435 N. Michigan Av., Magnificent Mile, subway Red Line to Grand*

Cookies By Design (O)
★ Sugary souvenirs for those with a sweet tooth, perhaps the most original of all Chicago souvenirs; freshly-baked biscuits which will stand the long flight home unharmed. They also come with logos on each one and can be given any inscription you wish. *1311 Golf Rd., Rolling Meadows (about a 45 minute journey), bus 208 to Golf Road*

Expressly Wood (106/C 3)
Items crafted in real wood: exotic souvenirs and accessories such as jewellery boxes, picture frames, clocks, toys and board games. *825 West Armitage Av., Lincoln Park, subway Red Line to Armitage*

Original Expressions (106/C 3)
Unusual gifts in all shapes and colours, nicely wrapped and tied with a decorative bow and accompanied by a cheerful greet-ings card. For those with extrava-gant tastes. *837 W. Armitage Av., Lincoln Park, subway Blue Line to Armitage*

SPORTS CLOTHING

NikeTown Chicago (109/D 2)
★ ☘ The successful chain of the well-known sports shoe firm has opened up in Chicago. All

(!) the Nike models of shoes and and accessories are there for your approval on several floors and half a basketball pitch. A paradise for kids! *Open Mon–Fri 10 am–8 pm, Sat 9.30 am–6 pm, Sun 10 am–6 pm, 669 N. Michigan Av., Mag-nificent Mile, subway Red Line to Chicago Street*

Sportmart (108/C 2)
Seven floors of sports goods by all kinds of companies. Its seven floors make it even bigger than Nike. On the ground floor all the Chicago Bulls merchandise is displayed, a must for Michael Jordan fans. *620 N. LaSalle St., River North, subway Red Line to Grand Avenue*

TOYS

FAO Schwarz (109/D 1)
☘ This well known toy chain, now a New York institution, has branches all over America. The Chicago branch offers a huge selection of toys spread over several floors. Children can touch and even try everything! *Open Mon–Thu 10 am–7 pm, Fri, Sat 10 am–8 pm, Sun 11 am–7 pm, 840 N. Michigan Av., Magnifi-cent Mile, subway Red Line to Chicago Street*

Saturday's Child (106/B 2)
Not as large as FAO Schwarz or Toys 'R Us, the toy super-chains, but more original. Here you can still buy rubber snakes, metal frogs and comical clocks which are normally found in chewing gum machines. *2146 N. Halsted St., Lincoln Park, subway Red Line to Fullerton*

A good night's sleep

From luxury suites to cheap suburban hotels – in the shadow of the skyscrapers everybody can find the accommodation of their choice

Chicago is a pricey place. In particular, hotel guests who travel privately to Chicago will find that out, whereas it matters little to business travellers. They go up to their rooms in the high-rise hotels on North Michigan Avenue, open their laptops and do not have to worry about the prices. The service for business travellers gets better and better, and there is even an hotel with its own FedEx letter-box. Modem points now go without saying.

All that is of little interest to the holidaymaker. All he wants is as comfortable a room as possible and friendly service for a reasonable price. Therefore, in the more expensive hotels, always ask about budget specials. That is perfectly in order in the USA, there are scarcely any hotels which do not have a cheaper weekly tariff or can magic some other form of discount from their computer. A prerequisite for an attractive quote is that there must

not be a convention in progress, because prices jump skyhigh at such times and you would be lucky to find even a tiny room at a horrific price. Newly available for a few years now are what are known as suite-hotels, with small suites of several rooms and a small kitchen annex suitable for families, and low budget hotels with very clean and adequately furnished rooms at an acceptable price including breakfast (albeit meagre).

Bear the following points in mind when reserving rooms (and do this as early as possible): prices are always for a double room but net of tax and possible parking fees. Singles sometimes get a discount. Rooms may have a king bed (kingsize), queen bed (normal double) or twin beds, as well as ensuite shower or bath. As a rule breakfast is not included in the price. Chicago hotels are cheapest between January and March –no wonder, for it is then that an icy wind blows down Michigan Avenue.

Hotel reservation over the internet: *www.hotrooms.com*

Many hotels offer enchanting views of Chicago at night

MARCO POLO SELECTION: HOTELS

1 Whitehall Hotel
Victorian elegance
combined with modern
comfort (page 63)

2 House of Blues Hotel
Modern technology in every
room (page 64)

3 Swissotel Chicago
Luxury hotel with a fine
view of the lake (page 66)

4 Tremont Hotel
Cheerful colours and a
fitness centre on the roof
(page 66)

5 Hotel Allegro
Bold design and excellent
service (page 63)

6 City Suites Hotel
A comfortable suburban
hotel in a lively quarter
(page 66)

7 Hampton Inn & Suites
Friendly hotel, cheap and
good (page 67)

8 Surf Hotel
Beautiful lobby and 1920s
furniture (page 67)

9 The Drake
The "Grand Dame of
Chicago" has its price
(page 65)

10 Hyatt Regency Chicago
The atrium lobby alone is
worth a visit (page 65)

HOTELS CATEGORY 1

(for the discriminating; from 200 dollars for a double room)

Chicago Marriott   **(109/D 3)**
This luxury hotel, with almost 200 rooms, has gone up a class following thorough renovation, even though this may possibly surprise the guests. Those who like giant and palatial hotels will find all they seek here. *1172 rooms, 540 N. Michigan Av., Magnificent Mile, Tel. 312/836 01 00, Fax 836 69 38, www.marriott.com, subway Red Line to Grand/State*

Doubletree Guest Suites (109/D 1)
Doubletree belongs to the high-class hotel chain with well appointed rooms and excellent service, but it will cost you 200 dollars a night. *345 rooms, 198 E. Delaware Place, Near North, Tel. 312/664 11 00, Fax 664 98 81, subway Red Line to Grand/State*

Inter-Continental Chicago   **(109/D 3)**
Two tower blocks at the southern end of the Magnificent Mile. The more southerly of the two was built in 1929 and offers classic elegance with its spacious rooms, while the northern one is more modern and traditionally appointed. The best of service. *844 rooms, 505 N. Michigan Av., Magnificent Mile, Tel. 312/944 41 00, Fax 944 13 20, www.inter-conti.com, subway Red Line to Grand/State*

Omni Chicago Hotel   **(109/D 2)**
Fresh flowers, burgundy-coloured wallpaper and shining marble floors everywhere – and the Magnificent Mile starts outside; just how you imagine a

luxury hotel to be. All the rooms are spacious suites, complete with kitchen, dining table and full bar. *347 rooms, 676 N. Michigan Av., Magnificent Mile, Tel. 312/944 66 64, Fax 266 30 i5, www.omnihotels.com, subway Red Line to Grand/State*

Renaissance Chicago Hotel (108/C 4)

✑ A top hotel on the northern edge of the Loop; through the panoramic window there is a superb view of the river and skyscrapers. The rooms on the Club Level are twice as large. The open sky can be seen through the large windows above the swimming pool. *553 roms, 1 W. Wacker Dr., on the Loop, Tel. 312/372 72 00, Fax 372 00 93, www.renaissancehotels.com, El Brown to State/Lake, subway Red Line to Washington/State*

The Silversmith (Crowne Plaza Chicago) (109/D 5)

Located in the former jewellers' trading centre, you would not appreciate the class of this luxury hotel from the outside. But the interior has been expensively renovated and the huge rooms are lavishly appointed. *143 rooms, 10 S. Wabash St., in the Loop, Tel. 312/372 76 96, Fax 372 73 20, www.crowneplaza.com, El Brown, Green, Orange to Madison/Wabash*

Talbott Hotel (109/D 1)

Built in 1920 as apartments for well-to-do families, a comfortable hotel since 1989 such as might be seen in Vienna or Paris. Huge rooms with all the extras – and, of course, the telephones have a modem link. *146 rooms, 20 E. Delaware Place, Near North, Tel.* *312/944 49 70, Fax 944 72 41, www.thetelbott.com, subway Red Line to Grand/State*

Whitehall Hotel (109/D 1)

★ An intimate luxury hotel in a former 1920s residence which has been expensively renovated. European elegance and modern comfort, the rooms are furnished in Victorian style. *221 rooms, 105 E. Delaware Place, Near North, Tel. 312/944 63 00, Fax 944 85 52, www.whitehallchicago.com, subway Red Line to Chicago/State*

HOTELS CATEGORY 2

(middle-class hotels, from 140 dollars for a double room)

Hotel Allegro (108/C 4)

★ Cheerful, sometimes even gaudy colours and highly imaginative and artistic design make this hotel a unique jewel. The rooms are rather small, but the service is satisfactory and the CD players in the rooms are not to be despised. *483 rooms, 171 W. Randolph St., in the Loop, Tel. 312/236 01 23, Fax 236 31 77, El (all lines) to Washington*

The Claridge (107/E 6)

The rooms are elegantly appointed, with open fires in ths suites. The service is excellent and little extras like warm cookies at bedtime and the morning paper at breakfast make the stay even more pleasant. It is easier here to ignore the noisy traffic. *163 rooms, 1244 N. Dearborn Av., Near North, Tel. 312/787 49 80, Fax 787 40 69, subway Red Line to Clark/Division*

Colourful design and music in the lifts: Hotel Allegro

Courtyard By Marriott Chicago Downtown (109/D 3)

Courtyard is the budget branch of the Marriott, still a fine hotel but more standard with its somewhat sober furnishings. The River North restaurants lie in the immediate vicinity, otherwise it is some way away from where the action is. *334 rooms, 30 E. Hubbard St., River North, Tel. 312/329 25 00, Fax 329 94 52, subway Red Line to Grand/State*

Days Inn Lake Shore Dr. (109/D 2)

Located on the bank of the lake and linked with Navy Pier by an underground corridor. The rooms were expensively revamped in 1999. There is an outside swimming pool and a sun terrace. The buffet breakfast is lavish. *578 rooms, 644 Lake Shore Dr., Near North, Tel. 312/943 92 00, Fax 255 44 11, subway Red Line to Grand/State*

Embassy Suites (109/D 2)

For 160 dollars you get a two-room suite with a fully equipped kitchen including a microwave. Breakfast (included in the price) is served in the atrium. Ideal for families, the suites can accommodate five people in comfort. *358 suites, 600 N. State St., River North, Tel. 312/943 38 00, Fax 943 76 29, subway Red Line to Grand/State*

Fairmont Hotel (109/E 4)

A top hotel in the centre of Chicago with first class restaurants and attentive service. The rooms are equipped with every conceivable high-tech gadget, but the supercomfortable beds are the most luxurious item of all. *692 rooms, 200 N. Columbus Dr., east of the Loop, Tel. 312/565 80 00, Fax 856 10 32, El Brown, Green, Orange to Randolph*

House of Blues Hotel (109/D 3)

★ A stylish mix of Gothic,

Indian, Moroccan and New Orleans influences in one theme hotel – very close by lies the House of Blues Restaurant. All rooms have video recorders, CD players, fax equipment and an internet link. *367 rooms, Dearborn Av., River North, Tel. 312/245 03 33, Fax 245 05 04, subway Red Line to Grand/State*

Midland Hotel   (108/C 5)
Located in the business district, somewhat aged but revamped for a lot of money and equipped with spacious rooms. European antiques in the lobby. *387 rooms, 172 W. Adams St., in the Loop, Tel. 312/332 12 00, Fax 312/ 332 59 09, El Brown to Quincy*

Palmer House Hilton   (109/D 4)
Sister hotel of the Astoria in New York, even though by no means as luxurious. In the 19th century it was the city's largest

Luxury Hotels in Chicago

The Drake   (109/D 1)
★ The "Grand Dame of Chicago" – a venerable hotel on Lake Michigan with elegant rooms and excellent service. Afternoon tea is served in the Palm Court just as it used to be in England. *535 rooms, 140 E. Walton Place, Tel. 312/787 22 00, Fax 787 14 31, www.hilton.com, subway Red Line to Chicago/State*

Four Seasons Hotel   (109/D 1)
The city's most expensive hotel with the most attentive service. International guests are greeted with a jet lag tea. Tastefully appointed rooms, marble baths, video recorders and much more. *343 rooms, 120 E. Delaware Place, Tel. 312/280 88 00, Fax 280 91 84, www.hyatt.com, subway Red Line to Chicago/State*

Hyatt Regency Chicago   (109/D 4)
★ The world's largest Hyatt Hotel with two supermodern tower blocks. Comfortably appointed; in every room there is a FedEx letterbox – just in case! The atrium lobby with its trees and panoramic windows is an attraction in itself! *2019 rooms, 151 E. Wacker Dr., Tel. 312/565 12 34, Fax 565 29 66, www.hyatt.com, El Brown, Green, Orange to Randolph*

Ritz-Carlton Chicago   (109/D 1)
The lobby alone is twelve storeys high. The Ritz offers every conceivable facility and does everything to maintain its position in the world's best list. Traditionally appointed rooms with every extra (fax equipment in the room), elegant bathrooms, *435 rooms, 160 E. Pearson St., Tel. 312/266 10 00, Fax 266 11 94, www.fourseasons.com, subway Red Line to Chicago/State*

hotel and even today – after thorough renovation – it is one of the top addresses. Fitness centre, sauna and five restaurants. *1639 rooms, 17 E. Monroe St., in the Loop, Tel. 312/726 75 00, Fax 917 17 07, subway Red Line to Monroe/State*

Summerfield Suites
Hotel (109/D 2)
Roomy suites in a recently revamped middle-class hotel, ideal for small families who do not want to dine in the restaurant all the time. Every suite has a kitchen, and a video recorder is standard equipment. Breakfast is included in the price. *120 rooms, 166 E. Superior St., Near North, Tel. 312/387 60 00, Fax 787 61 33, subway Red Line to Chicago/State*

Swissotel Chicago (109/E 4)
★ ⬇ The hotel with the finest view over Lake Michigan and Grant Park. Large modern rooms and a unique fitness centre on the roof. There is a 9-hole golf course nearby. *632 rooms, 323 E. Wacker Dr., east of the Loop, Tel. 312/565 05 65, Fax 565 99 30, El Brown, Green, Orange to Randolph*

Tremont Hotel (109/D 1)
★ A former 1920s residence and since the 1970s – following an expensive revamp – a comfortable hotel in the European style. Cheerful colours in the *130 rooms. 100 E. Chestnut St., Near North, Tel. 312/751 19 00, Fax 751 86 91, subway Red to Chicago/State*

HOTELS CATEGORY 3

(middle-class hotels, from 80 dollars for a double room)

Best Western Grant Park (111/D 4)
Budget hotel with standard rooms. The morning coffee which you make yourself and a morning paper are included, and use of the fitness room is free. Please ask for cheap weekend specials. *172 rooms, 1100 S. Michigan Av., east of the Loop, Tel. 312/922 29 00, Fax 922 88 12, subway Red Line to Roosevelt/State*

Blackstone Hotel (111/D 3)
288 very spacious and traditionally furnished rooms in an old, recently renovated multi-storey building which has a certain charm. Some scenes from the film "The Untouchables" were shot here. *636 S. Michigan Av., east of the Loop, Tel. 312/427 43 00, Fax 427 47 36, subway Red Line to Harrison/State*

City Suites Hotel (O)
★ A comfortable suburban hotel in a former residence, the small suites are very pleasantly appointed. Interesting bars and restaurants in the vicinity. *45 suites, 933 W. Belmont Av., North Side, Tel. 773/404 34 00, Fax 404 34 05, subway Blue Line to Belmont*

Congress Plaza Hotel (111/D 2)
This large hotel is centrally located at Grant Park. The Buckingham Fountain and Lake Michigan are just outside the door. The cosy furnishings and friendly service make up for the dull exterior. *852 rooms, 520 S. Michigan Av., east of the Loop, Tel. 312/427 38 00, Fax 312/427 72 64, subway Red Line to Harrison/State*

Essex Inn (111/D 3)

Very simple and cheap hotel with attractive offers on price. With some "specials" you get a ticket to the Chicago Bears (otherwise hard to obtain). *255 rooms, 800 S. Michigan Av., east of the Loop, Tel. 312/939 28 00, Fax 922 61 53, subway Red Line to Harrison*

Hampton Inn & Suites (108/C 3)

★ This chain is known for its bright and suitably appointed rooms, with enlarged old picture postcards on the walls. Swimming pool and sauna in the hotel, breakfast and morning coffee free of charge. *230 rooms/suites. 33 W. Illinois St., River North, Tel. 312/832 03 30, Fax 832 03 33, subway Red Line to Grand/State*

Hotel Monaco (109/D 4)

A tastefully and colourfully appointed hotel which only opened in 1998 and is very popular because of its central location. *193 rooms, 225 N. Wabash Av., on the Loop, Tel. 312/960 85 00, Fax 960 18 83, buses 2, 10, 146 to Wabash Avenue*

Lenox Suites Hotel (109/D 2)

A plain hotel with practical furniture, but centrally located. The Mag Mile shops are just a few streets away. The budget rooms are very simple, the better ones fall into Category 2. *325 rooms, 616 N. Rush St., Near North, Tel. 312/337 10 00, Fax 337 72 17, subway Red Line to Grand/State*

Motel 6 (109/D 2)

The only hotel of this well known chain in the city centre, known for its sparsely furnished but very clean rooms at very favourable prices. There is even a restaurant. For those who must be economical or prefer to spend their money in other ways. *191 rooms, 162 E. Ontario St., Near North, Tel. 312/787 35 80, Fax 787 12 99, subway Red Line to Grand/State*

Ohio House Motel (108/C 3)

Clean and simple, but located on the Gold Coast near the clubs and restaurants. You are not likely to find better value anywhere in the city centre. *50 rooms, 600 N. LaSalle St., Near North, Tel. 312/943 60 00, Fax 943 60 63, subway Red Line to Grand/State*

Surf Hotel (O)

★ A romantic suburban hotel with an impressive lobby and small but comfortable rooms. 1920s antiques. Breakfast is included in the price. *45 rooms, 555 Surf St., Wrigleyville, Tel. 773/528 84 00, Fax 528 84 83, bus 156 to Sheridan/Surf*

YOUTH HOSTELS/GUEST HOUSES

Arlington House International Hostel (106/C 1)

A youth hostel at Lincoln Park with single rooms (about US$ 40) and shared rooms (about US$ 20), open all the year. *616 W. Arlington Place, Tel. 312/929 53 80, Fax 665 54 85, subway/El Red, Brown, Purple to Fullerton*

International House of Chicago (O)

Cheap rooms (about US$ 40) in Hyde Park on the campus of the University of Chicago. *1414 E. 59th St., Tel. 773/753 22 70, Fax 753 12 27, bus 55 to University of Chicago, El Green to Garfield*

Chicago diary

Magnificently colourful parades and imaginative street celebrations are features of the Chicago festival calendar

Each ethnic minority celebrates its own festival; without the Mexicans, Chinese, Irish and Afro-Americans the Windy City's festival diary would look much less interesting. Culture, music and merry street parties make winter much more bearable, and even the weakest rays of sunshine will then entice the inhabitants of Chicago out onto the streets. So the great number of street parties and cultural events comes as no surprise. Every opportunity is taken to dance in the open air, sing and eat. Art is inherent among the people; instead of flea markets like those held in other towns Chicago offers literature, painting and other arts. Chicago does not have just one scene but many, one on every street corner, and during the street parties the artists fraternise with passers by.

You can obtain a brochure giving details of all the festivals and events from the *Chicago Office of Tourism*. The *Special Events Hot Line, Tel. 312/744 33 70*, also provides information

about the major dates and programmes.

PUBLIC HOLIDAYS

All public offices, banks and many shops are closed on the following days: *New Year's Day* (1 January), *Martin Luther King Jr. Day* (third Monday in January), *President's Day* (third Monday in February), *Memorial Day* (last Monday in May), *Independence Day* (4 July), *Labor Day* (first Monday in September), *Columbus Day* (second Monday in October), *Veterans Day* (11 November), *Thanksgiving* (last Thursday in November), *Christmas Day* (25 December)

FESTIVALS, EVENTS, FAIRS

February
Black History Month
Numerous events, talks and shows relating to Afro-American history in the *Chicago Cultural Center*, in the *Museum of Science and Industry* and in the *Du Sable Museum of African-American History*

Chinese New Year Parade
In Chinatown the clocks work differently, so to speak, and according to the Chinese calendar

Parades like this are arranged year after year by all ethnic groups

The Blues Festival on the lawns of Grant Park lasts for three days

the New Year is not celebrated until February. The Chinese in Chicago celebrate the coming of the New Year with the traditional dragons and a magnificently colourful procession through the Chinese quarter.

March
St Patrick's Day Parade
★ On the Saturday closest to 17 March the Irish really paint the town red. This Irish national holiday is celebrated in the Windy City with a noisy procession along Dearborn Street.

June
Ravinia Festival
The Chicago Symphony Orchestra and other ensembles, artistes and ballet companies perform in Ravinia Park on Chicago's North Shore. *For tickets: Tel. 847/266 51 00, Highland Park, suburban train to Highland Park*

Chicago Blues Festival
★ On the *first weekend in June* the "city of the blues" celebrates its music. The Blues Festival is one of the country's major musical events and every year attracts fans from all over the world. And the best thing is that admission is free to the open-air concerts in the Petrillo Music Shell. *Grant Park, buses 3, 4, 6, 60, 145, 147, 151 to Grant Park*

Gay and Lesbian Pride Parade
★ Love parade à la Chicago – not as large and colourful as in Berlin, for example, but still impressive. On the last Sunday in June gays and lesbians proceed from Halsted Street to Lincoln Park, where an open-air concert is held.

Printers Row Book Fair
Printers Row *(Dearborn Street, between Congress and Polk Street)* is known in Chicago for its good

range of bookshops. In the *first week in June* new and antique books are on sale in the open, and readings by authors take place in a tent. *Printers Row, subway Red Line to Harrison*

July

Fiesta del Sol

The Mexicans celebrate in July. Their fiesta, a large popular festival with roundabouts and hotdog stalls, is held in Pilsen between 18th and 22nd Streets. *Subway Blue Line to 18th St., end of July*

August

Northhalsted Market Days

★ Large street festival on Halsted Street between Belmont Avenue and Addison Street. Live music on several stages, numerous stands selling craftwork and fast food. *Subway Blue Line to Belmont Avenue*

Chicago Air & Water Show

Daredevil men in flying "crates" and (almost) flying boats in front of and over North Avenue Beach. For details of programme: *Tel. 312/744 33 15, bus 72 to Lincoln Park*

September

Around the Coyote

Action in the new artists' quarter; every second weekend in September the artists' enclave in Wicker Park and Bucktown opens the doors of its studios and the artists celebrate with the visitors. *Subway Blue Line to Damen*

October

Chicago International Film Festival

Alternative and independent films (*low budget*, without big backers and distributors) are shown in various cinemas in the city. The festival begins on the *first Thursday in October* and lasts two weeks. *Programme: Tel. 312/425 94 00*

November

Magnificent Mile Lights Festival

The Americans love parades and bright lights. At this event they get both; illuminated Disney characters meet Father Christmas on the *Mag Mile*, and shopowners give away gifts of chocolate. *Subway Red Line to Chicago/State, Saturday before Thanksgiving*

MARCO POLO SELECTION: EVENTS

1 St Patrick's Day Parade
Chicago River is painted green on the day of this Irish festival (page 70)

2 Chicago Blues Festival
Chicago celebrates its music with fans from all over the world (page 70)

3 Gay and Lesbian Pride Parade
Love parade ... la Chicago (page 70)

4 Northhalsted Market Days
Probably the city's most entertaining street festival (page 71)

Out on the town

Chicago is famous for its top quality cultural events and unusual subcultural haunts

Chicago is a cosmopolitan city and an important cultural metropolis. You will also find that in the evenings, when the sun goes down and the floodlit skyscrapers are bathed in candy-coloured light. Behind the illuminated façades and in the noisy streets of the Old Town the spotlight falls on actors, singers, dancers and other artistes, and the lively Windy City scene awakens to a new life. And even though the city's best-known cabaret act is called "The Second City", Chicago can still hold its own with New York at night too, and some ensembles and troupes make the "Big Apple" (as New York is known) look somewhat old. Nightclubs and subcultural haunts can be found in the Loop as well as in such "in" districts as Wicker Park and River North. This city on the east coast surely has the better discos.

But anyone coming to Chicago will also hear other music: blues, above all authentic blues (it is often claimed to be the true home of the blues), and (alternative)

Chicago's music scene is very wide: blues "greats" perform at the Kingston Mines Club

rock. Some of the best groups come from Chicago, the Smashing Pumpkins, Urge Overkill, Poi Dog Pondering and, of course, Chicago, the supergroup named after the city. Particularly with its alternative theatrical groups such as Steppenwolf and its high-class opera, with its open-air concerts which are held in the city parks in the summer and other cultural institutions. Chicago is very competitive as regards art and entertainment.

BARS & NIGHTCLUBS

Berlin (O)
Actually a chic gay bar, with the relevant music (Frankie Goes to Hollywood lives on!) and freaked out waiters, but it is also very popular with heteros. Prince and other favourites perform on giant video screens. *Open from midnight onwards, 954 W. Belmont Av., North Side, subway Blue Line to Belmont*

Big Chicks (O)
Gays, lesbians and creative heteros all feel at ease in this bar owned by the singer Michelle Fire. Her pictures hang on the walls. There is dancing at weekends, and on Sundays there are tasty morsels to

be had from the free buffet. *5024 N. Sheridan Rd., Lincoln Park, subway Red Line to Argyle*

Big Brasserie and Bar (109/D 4)
★ ☺ A giant bar in the atrium lobby of the (almost) futuristic Hyatt Regency with exquisite wines and rare brands of whisky including some from Britain. A super view of the city at night. *Open daily 11 am–2 am, 151 E. Wacker Dr., Loop, El Brown, Orange, Green to Randolph Street*

CroBar Night Club (109/A 4)
A temple of hip hop and technology in a warehouse quarter by Lincoln Park. The decor would suit a murky science fiction film. The city's largest dance floor. Drag queens appear on Sundays and (sometimes) the basketball star Dennis Rodman shows up.

Open Wed–Sun 9 pm–4 am, 1543 N. Kingsbury Court, Near North, bus 72 to Lincoln Park.

Drink (108/A 4)
★ The city's most interesting and probably largest club. Guests can enjoy themselves in the former storage rooms, dance to rock 'n' roll tunes of the seventies and drink from buckets and babys' bottles. Six bars (one serves 50 different brands of vodka) and a Cigar Room for smokers. *Open Mon 11.30 am–2.30 pm, Tue, Wed 11.30 am–2 am, Thu, Fri 11.30 am–4 am, Sat 5.30 pm–4 am, 702 W. Fulton St., Near West, El Green to Clinton*

Excalibur Entertainment Complex (108/C 2)
The name says it all. In this Roman-styled club everything is

MARCO POLO SELECTION: NIGHT-LIFE

1 Big Brasserie and Bar
A regal bar in the atrium lobby of the Hyatt (page 74)

2 Drink
Where the drinks are served in buckets and babys' bottles (page 74)

3 The Second City
Top class political cabaret (page 76)

4 Music Box Theatre
A little jewel box from the 1920s (page 76)

5 B.L.U.E.S.
The blues is regularly celebrated here (page 77)

6 Kingston Mines
A classic among blues clubs with two stages (page 78)

7 New Checkerboard Lounge
Where the Mississippi flows through Chicago (page 79)

8 Hubbard St. Dance
Jazz dancing to perfection (page 77)

9 Lyric Opera of Chicago
Opera can hardly get any better than this! (page 79)

10 Steppenwolf Theatre Company
John Malkovich and other famous actors live on stage (page 79)

High life of all kinds is on offer at the Excalibur Entertainment Complex

geared to size. The Chicago Tribune voted this complex of discos and games rooms as the best club in the city, although for some natives it is too cosmopolitan and touristy. Everything is done to provide entertainment. *Open Sun–Fri 4 pm–4 am, Sat 4 pm–5 am, 632 N. Dearborn St., Near North, bus 22 to Ontario Street*

Hopleaf (O)

College kids and refined yuppies patronise this chic bar in Wrigleyville, flip through the pages of "in scene" magazines, listen to the strange mixture of country, jazz and rhythm and blues music and drink one of the 100 and more types of beer. This is the place for those who like things a bit quieter. *5148 N. Clark St., Wrigleyville, subway Red Line to Berwyn*

The Matchbox (O)

An Irish pub and popular with the members of the Steppenwolf Theatre Company opposite. The writers and would-be authors who also patronise it like the dark Guiness and the photos of poets on the walls. *700 N. Milwaukee, Wear North, Buses 8, 65 to Grant Avenue*

O'Rourkes (106/B4)

Irish pub and popular meeting place for the creative set of the Steppenwolf Theatre Company. Writers and would-be writers also frequent this pub and enjoy a Guiness and the photographs of poets on the walls. *1625 N. Halsted St., Old Town, bus 72 to Halsted*

Red Dog (O)

Under the roof of an old residence in the new "in" quarter of Wicker Park lies what is probably the most popular underground club in the city. On Mondays gays and other colourful characters celebrate in the Boom Boom Room. *1958 W. North Av., Wicker Park, subway Blue Line to Damen*

Roscoe's Tavern (O)
Old-fashioned shop with a large bar, pool tables and an excellent dance floor; snacks are served on the patio. Also popular with the gays of the neighbourhood. *[3356 N. Halsted St., Lincoln Park, subway Red Line to Belmont Avenue*

Sidetrack (O)
A somewhat dark shed in which video fans apparently like being bombarded with the latest clips from several screens at once. The loud alternative to Roscoe's opposite. *3349 N. Halsted St., Lincoln Park, subway Red Line to Belmont Avenue*

Tania's (O)
Latin music in a restaurant which converts to a dinner club in the late evening. You can dance to rhythmic salsa sounds and sway to the rumba. *Open Fri, Sat from 10.30 pm, 2659 Milwaukee Av., North Side, bus 56 to Kedze Avenue*

CINEMAS

Music Box Theatre (O)
★ A jewel from the 1920s. Just to see this historic cinema with its pretty stucco decoration and magnificently coloured pictures makes the visit worthwhile. Its programme includes foreign and altenative films. *3733 N. Southport Av., Tel. 773/871 66 04, Lincoln Park, subway Red Line to Addison*

600 N. Michigan (109/D2)
The largest cinema complex in Chicago with a number of auditoriums and the best sound. Here the greatest Hollywood films are shown and also the Chicago International Film Festival is screened here. *600 N. Michigan Av., subway Red Line to Chicago Street*

CLASSICAL MUSIC

Chicago Symphony Orchestra (109/D 5)
An institution in Chicago since 1891 and a rise to world fame under Georg Solti. It has made over 900 albums and won over 50 Grammy awards and stands at the top of the classic charts. Each season it concentrates on one great master composer. In summer the orchestra plays in the open air at the Ravinia festival in Highland Park. *Symphony Center, 220 S. Michigan Av., Loop, Tel. 312/294 30 00, buses 3, 4, 14, 60, 145, 147, 151 and El (all lines) to Adams Street*

COMEDY

All Jokes Aside (110/C 3)
Only for those familiar with the American dialect: Afro-Ameri-can and Latin American humour from first-class comedians. *Open Wed–Sun from 6 pm, 1000 S. Wabash Av., buses 1, 3, 4 to 9th St., Near South, El Green, Orange to Roosevelt/State*

The Second City (107/D 4)
★ The top venue for political satire since 1959, the "Second City" is said to be second only to New York. Bitter humour, first class presenters. Numerous

members of ensembles (for example, John Malcovich) have made a career as film stars. *Open Mon–Thu 8.30 pm, Fri, Sat 8 and 10.30 pm, Sun 8 pm, 1616 N. Wells St., Old Town, bus 72 to N. Wells Street*

DANCING

Hubbard Street Dance (111/D 2)
★ The troupe began in 1977 in a small studio in Hubbard Street and graduated into one of the best in the country. Highly imaginative choreography, jazz dancing cannot get much better. *50 E. Congress Av., Grant Park, tickets: Tel. 312/902 15 00, buses 2, 7, 10, 126, 146 to Congress*

The Joffrey Ballet of Chicago (111/D 2)
Modern ballet to perfection. The ensemble came originally from New York and appears in the same theatre as the Hubbard Street Dance. *50 E. Congress Av., Grant Park, tickets: Tel. 312/902 15 00, buses 2, 7, 10, 126, 146 to Congress*

MUSIC BARS

Blue Chicago (108/C 2)
One of the best blues clubs in the city, furnished in 1940s style. The low admission charges are also enticing. Above all, the Queens of the Blues appear here. *Open Mon–Sat 8 pm–2 am, 736 N. Clark St., Near North, bus 125 to Clark Street*

B.L.U.E.S. (106/B 1)
★ The New York Times, of all people, has described this club as a "gold mine". Admittedly seating is a bit cramped, but equally you sit very close to the little stage as a result. *Open daily from 9 pm, 2519 N. Halsted St., Near North, El Brown, Purple and subway Red Line to Fullerton*

The true music of the city can also be heard in the Blue Chicago

Jam sessions and improvisation keep the music alive

Buddy Guy's Legends (110/C 3)

Buddy Guy is one the best blues guitarists. Some famous colleagues and gifted newcomers play here, and the walls are covered with blues memorabilia. *Open Mon–Thu 5 pm–2 am, Fri 4 pm–2 am, Sat 5 pm–3 am, Sun 6 pm–2 am, 754 S. Wabash Av., south of the Loop, subway Red Line to Harrison*

Double Door (O)

Previously a bikers' dosshouse where bands such as Marshall Tucker performed their swansong, today it is a recognised club for rock and alternative rock. Very good accoustics! Live appearances from 9 pm onwards. *1572 N. Milwaukee Av., Wicker Park, subway Blue Line to Damen*

Equator Club (O)

African and Caribbean sounds in this atmospheric cellar club. The music comes mostly from CDs, but sometimes live bands appear. Live shows from 8 pm. *4715 N. Broadway, North Side, subway Red Line to Lawrence*

Kingston Mines (106/B 1)

★ One of the best known blues clubs for more than 30 years, and even musicians come here to join the audience. Music is played alternately on two stages. The actor George Clooney (the American hospital series "E.R." is filmed in Chicago) has been seen here. *Open Fri 8 pm–4 am, Sat 8 pm–5 am, 2548 N. Halsted St., Near North, El Brown, Purple and subway Red Line to Fullerton*

Metro (O)

Do not be deceived by the dilapidated building: Metro is one of the city's best rock clubs. The bands REM and Smashing Pumpkins started here. Newcomers are allowed to play once a week. *Open daily from 6.30 pm,*

3730 N. Clark St., Wrigleyville,
subway Red Line to Addison

New Checkerboard Lounge (O)
★ Somewhat remotely located in
South Side, but held in high
esteem by connoisseurs of the
blues, it was here that the Mississippi blues was first played.
*Open daily from 9.30 pm, 423 E.
43rd St., South Side, bus 43 to 43rd
Street*

Old Town School of Folk
Music (O)
For over 40 years a first-class
school for folk musicians and
host to the cream of folk and
bluegrass music. *Programme information: Tel. 773/525 77 93, 4533
N. Lincoln Av., North Side, bus 11.
El Brown to Montrose*

Wild Hare (O)
In the shadow of Wrigley Field
lies the self-styled "reggae capital
of America". First-class bands
from Jamaica stoke up the
Caribbean atmosphere. *Open
daily from 9.30 pm, 3530 N. Clark
St., Wrigleyville, subway Red Line to
Addison*

THEATRE, OPERA, MUSICALS

Ford Center for the
Performing Arts (108/C 4)
The Oriental Theatre, one of the
historic cinemas in the Loop
(built 1929) was expensively
restored and reopened in 1920s
style. A nostalgic ambience for
well known Broadway musicals.
*24 W. Randolph St., Loop, tickets:
Tel. 312/855 94 00, El (all lines) to
Randolph*

Goodman Theatre (109/D 5)
One of Chicago's oldest and best

theatres offering interesting productions of both classic and new
plays. Well-known actors regularly appear here. There are
plans to open a new Goodman
in the Loop in the year 2000.
*200 S. Columbus Dr., Grant Park,
Tel. 312/443 38 00, buses 1, 7. 126
to Art Institute, El (all lines) to
Adams*

Lyric Opera of Chicago (108/B 5)
★ Expensive   productions   of
well-known operas with world
stars like Placido Domingo and
Jesse Norman. More rare are
original productions of new plays
by   young   American   authors.
Tickets for the Lyric Opera are
extremely hard to obtain so you
should book well in advance
*Civic Opera House, Near West, Tel.
312/332 22 44, buses 14, 20, 56,
157 to Civic Opera House*

Steppenwolf Theatre
Company (106/B 4)
★ An excellent ensemble renowned both for its plays from
the traditional repertoire and its
brave performances. For many
critics the Steppenwolf Theatre
ranks among the best in the
USA. The acoustics are breathtaking. *1630 N. Halsted St., Old
Town, Tel. 312/335 16 50, bus 72
to N. Halsted, subway Red Line to
North/Clybourn*

Victory Gardens Theater (106/B 1)
Founded   in   the   1970s,   this
theatre is considerably more conservative than the Steppenwolf
but still very interesting because
plays by Chicago writers are performed by Chicago actors. *2257
N. Lincoln Av., Near North, Tel.
773/871 30 00, El Brown, Purple,
Orange to Fullerton*

Between the Mississippi and Lake Erie

Motor racing and historic little townships, farmland and wide sand-dune beaches – the variety of the countryside around Chicago is quite amazing

Fancy a beach holiday deep in the heart of the continent? A walk along a rocky coast, a pleasant catfish meal on the banks of the mighty Mississippi? Or perhaps you would prefer a visit to "Motown" Detroit with the highly polished veteran cars made by Henry Ford? The region around the Great Lakes can offer all this and still keep some surprises up its sleeve. The states bordering on the lakes – Ohio (OH), Indiana (IN), Michigan (MI), Illinois (IN), Wisconsin (WI) and Minnesota (MN) may not be as dramatic as those in the West but their many smaller attractions will still make your holiday charming.

A delightful and soft green landscape similar to that of central Europe stretches over the Ice Age hills around the Great Lakes.

From Chicago you can visit picture book villages like Galena here

Giant farms to the south, seemingly unending forest regions to the north, magnificent sanddunes along nearly 600 kilometres of shoreline, beaches and rocky bays. And in between lie picturesque holiday and fishing villages, fine golf resorts and quiet walking areas. So it is a land for explorers who will come across such intriguing regions as Amish Country in Indiana, where farmers of German descent live simple and God-fearing lives just as their ancestors did 200 years ago.

There are some interesting excursions from Chicago which can be completed in a rented car in one or two days, such as a trip to a spa in the Indiana dunes near Michigan City or a nostalgic drive along Route 66 to Springfield and St Louis in the neighbouring state of Missouri (MO). Other destinations may mean trips lasting several days: Mackinac Island, for instance, the idyllic Door Peninsula in Wisconsin or the historic little towns of Galena or Hannibal on the Mississippi, Mark Twain's home town. In order really to get to know the region around the Great Lakes you should allow yourself at least two or three weeks and undertake an extensive round trip by hired car. This is best in high summer if you have children with you and wish to bathe, otherwise the quieter spring and autumn with its magnificent colours are good times to travel. (For detailed information see Marco Polo volume "Eastern Canada").

CLEVELAND, OH

(115/F 4) For a long time this industrial city (Pop. 2,900,000 in the metropolitan area) was dominated by steel foundries and ugly port areas. In the early 19th century Cleveland was an important American industrial and commercial centre. The Second World War was followed by a long period of decline, but more recently the town has become attractive once more. The *Waterfront* on the banks of the lake and old warehouse areas such as *The Flats* on the Cuyahoga River were restored, in the *University Circle* quarter a number of excellent museums were built, and Christoph von Dohnányi made the Cleveland Orchestra world-famous.

The finest point from which to obtain a view over the city is the viewing platform on the 42nd floor of the *Terminal Tower* in the city centre. Immediately opposite, it is worth taking

MARCO POLO SELECTION: THE GREAT LAKES

1 Amish Country
Excursion to some peaceful, old-fashioned farming country (page 93)

2 Cahokia Mounds
Traces of an ancient Indian civilization (page 93)

3 House on the Rocks
Eccentric collection by a visionary (page 94)

4 Henry Ford Museum
The oldest Model-T Ford and many other veteran cars (page 84)

5 Mackinac Island
A nostalgic summer break like in the good old days (page 88)

6 Rock and Roll Hall of Fame
Everything about rock music – from Elvis to Jimi Hendrix (page 83)

7 Sleeping Bear Dunes
Dunes like those in the Sahara – up to 140 m high (page 95)

8 Taliesin
A shrine to Frank Lloyd Wright, America's most famous architect (page 94)

a look in the superbly decorated *Arcade* (*401 Euclid Avenue*) which dates from 1890 – one of America's first shopping arcades.

MUSEUMS

Cleveland Museum of Art
One of the best art museums in the New World. Particularly interesting is the medieval collection with many items from the Welfen treasures. *Open Tue–Sun 10 am–5 pm, admission free, 11150 East Boulevard*

Rock and Roll Hall of Fame
★ Right on the bank of the lake is a bold building by the star architect I.M. Pei, inside are memorabilia of famous bands and an exhibition on the history of rock music, *Open daily 10 am–5.30 pm, until 9 pm on Wed, admission US$ 14.95, 9th St./Erieside Avenue*

RESTAURANT

Watermark
◁▷ Good fish and a nice terrace in the harbour quarter, The Flats. [*1250 Old River Rd., Tel. 216/241 16 00, Category 2*

HOTEL

Glidden House
Ideal for those keen on art: an historic inn opposite the Museum of Art. *52 rooms, 1901 Ford Dr., Tel. 216/231 89 00, Fax 231 21 30, Category 2*

SURROUNDING AREA

Sandusky (115/E 4)
This holiday resort on Lake Erie is the place for those with children or who like roller coasters.

In the giant *Cedar Point* amusement park there are twelve of the largest, fastest and steepest *roller coasters* in the world. *Open daily May–beginning of Sep*

DETROIT, MI

(**115/E 4**) Sooty factories and rundown residential areas are the first things you notice when you enter the most important city (Pop. 5,300,000) in the state of Michigan. At the same time this city on the Detroit River, which here forms the border with Canada, has won a big reputation as America's motor car capital. It was here that Henry Ford invented the conveyor belt and Thomas Edison built the world's first electric power station and the first traffic lights appeared. The gigantic motor car factories of General Motors, Ford and Chrysler can still be found here today. A city which can be proud of its achievements.

However, bitter strikes in the factories, racial unrest and a high crime rate have given Detroit a bad image. Only in the last few years have marked changes been made; many slum districts have been cleared and Downtown by the Detroit River, formerly completely desolate, has been given a new lease of life.

SIGHTS

The best sightseeing tour for gaining an initial impression costs only 50 cents: it is a round trip on the *Detroit People Mover*, a fully automatic elevated railway, around the city centre. Worthwhile stops include the ◁▷ *Renaissance Center*, built of reflecting glass cylinders,

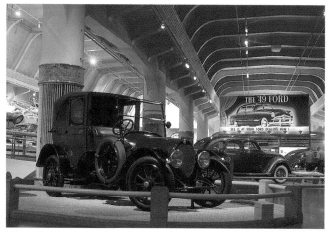

Henry Ford Museum, where the heart of any motor car freak will beat faster.

(viewing platform and revolving restaurant) and *Greektown*, the colourful restaurant quarter around Monroe Street. Somewhat further west on Woodward Avenue, the city's main traffic artery, lies Detroit's cultural district with the campus of *Wayne State University* and the art museum *Detroit Institute of Arts (5200 Woodward Av.)* which, besides owning such masterpieces as Pieter Breughel's "Village Wedding", also has some very interesting monumental paintings of Detroit by Diego Riviera.

Also worth a visit is *Belle Isle Park* on an island in the Detroit River with a large aquarium and the *Dossin Great Lakes Museum*, which documents shipping on the lakes. The "in" quarter around *Main Street* in the suburb of ✱ *Royal Oak* is ideal for a stroll. The "lovely young people" frequent the street cafés and pubs and blues and rock music blares forth from the open bar windows.

Henry Ford Museum

★ With dozens of veteran cars this museum documents the history of the motor car industry and technology of America. Adjoining it is *Greenfield Village*, an open air museum with 80 historic houses such as the Wright Brothers' cycle shop and Thomas Edison's laboratory. You can enjoy a break in one of the restaurants. *Open daily 9 am–5 pm, admission US$ 12.50, museum and village US$ 22, Village Rd./Oakwood Bd., Dearborn*

Motown Museum

From 1959 to 1972 this simple house was the recording studio of such Motown stars as Smokey Robinson, Diana Ross and the Supremes. *Open Tue–Sat 10 am–5 pm, Sun, Mon from midday, admission US$ 6, 2648 W. Grand Boulevard*

Museum of African American History

A large museum complex illustrating the fate of blacks in America from the days of slavery to the present day. *Tue–Sun 9.30 am–5 pm, admission US$ 3, 315 E. Warren Avenue*

Franklin Street Brewery

⚡ A popular "in" place in the Rivertown nightlife quarter; good fish and pasta dishes. *Open daily from 6 pm, 1560 Franklin St., Tel. 313/568 03 90, Category 2*

Memphis Smoke

❂ Spare ribs and good solid Southern States food in the Royal Oak "hip" district; blues bands from 10 pm. *100 S. Main St., Tel. 248/543 43 00, Category 2–3*

The Whitney

An elegant dinner restaurant in a Victorian villa on the western edge of the city centre. Popular for business meals, very good wine menu. *Open Mon–Fri 11 am–2 pm, 5–9 pm, Sat 5–10 pm, Sun 5–8 pm, 4421 Woodward Av., Tel. 313/832 57 00, Category 1–2*

Atheneum Suite Hotel

A modern tower building with 174 suites; good restaurant with cajun cuisine; the "Fishbone Rhythm Kitchen Café", *1000 Brush St., Tel. 313/962 23 23, Fax 962 24 24, Category 1–2*

Hampton Inn Dearborn

A modern but simple chain hotel near the Henry Ford Museum. *119 rooms, 20061 Michigan Av., Tel.* *313/ 436 96 00, Fax 436 83 45, Category 3*

Detroit Visitor Center

211 W. Fort St., Detroit, MI 48 226, Tel. 313/202 18 00, Fax 202 18 34, www.visitdetroit.com

GALENA, IL

(114/B 4) This charming little historic township (Pop. 4,000) on a branch of the Mississippi possessed the most important harbour north of St Louis during the 19th century. Paddle steamers moored here and lead was shipped in by giant freighters from the mines in the surrounding areas. However, the harbour then silted up and Galena fell into a Sleeping Beauty type sleep. It was not until recent years that this well preserved gem from Civil War days was rediscovered. The ornamental old brick houses on *Main Street* were restored and restaurants, art galleries and shops opened up. And today the magnificent sea-captains' villas on the slopes above the Galena River house nostalgic country inns and bed and breakfast accommodation.

With the help of old photographs the little *Galena History Museum (211 Bench St.)* explains the history of the town, while the splendidly decorated *Belvedere Mansion (1008 Park Av.)* of 1857 gives an insight into the life of a rich ship owner in the 19th century. It is also worthwhile taking a drive through the hilly countryside hereabouts with its apple plantations and little forests. Picture-book villages like *Scales Mound* or *Warren* reflect rural life in the mid-West.

HOTEL/GUEST HOUSE

DeSoto House Hotel

A renovated hotel dating from 1855 in the Old Town. *55 rooms, 230 S. Main St., Tel. 815/777 00 90, Fax 777 95 29, Category 2–3*

Park Avenue Guest House

A well-run bed and breakfast establishment in an 1897 Victorian house, quiet location but near the Old Town. *4 rooms, 208 Park Av., Tel. 815/777 10 75, Fax 777 10 97, Category 2–3*

SURROUNDING AREA

Dubuque **(114/B 4)**
Another old port, but Dubuque lies directly on the banks of the Mississippi in the neighbouring state of Iowa. From ↘ *Eagle Point Park* a cliff offers a magnificent view over the river and of *General Pike Dam*. In the Old Town there are still many classic houses to be found in Locust Street and Bluff Street which date from Dubuque's heyday when it became wealthy as a result of lead mining.

GREEN BAY, WI

(114/C 2) Every child in America knows Green Bay, because it is the home town of the "Packers", a legendary football team which has already won the US championship several times. You should visit the *Hall of Fame (Open daily 10 am–5 pm)* opposite the stadium on Lombardi Street.

However, Green Bay also has a history; it is one of the oldest white settlements on the Great Lakes – founded by a French Jesuit missionary in 1669. The timber industry and commerce made the town wealthy. The life of the pioneers is portrayed in the *Heritage Hill State Park* open air museum on Highway 172, while the unhappy saga of the Indians is told in the *Oneida Nation Museum* on the reserve west of the town. On the southern edge of town there is a special treat in store for lovers of steam locomotives: the *National Railroad Museum, 2285 S. Broadway* has some 70 old trains and coaches on display.

HOTEL

James St. Inn

A fine country hotel in the suburb of De Pere and located in an old corn mill on the banks of the Fox River. *30 rooms, 201 James St., De Pere, Tel. 920/ 337 01 11, Fax 337 61 35, Category 2–3*

SURROUNDING AREA

Door Peninsula **(114/C 2)**
This long peninsula north-east of Green Bay is probably Wisconsin's most popular holiday region. Rugged rocky cliffs, picturesque bays for bathing and cute harbour towns like those in New England are dotted along the shoreline, while inland large cherry plantations cover the hills in spring with a carpet of white flowers. A superb place for cycle tours and pleasant days spent walking along the shore or

enjoying fish dinners, The most beautiful villages are *Bayley's Harbor, Egg Harbor* and *Fish Creek. Whitefish Dunes State Park* offers a peaceful spot for bathing. The island's capital is Sturgeon Bay (Pop. 10,000). *Information: Door County Chamber of Commerce, 1012 Green Bay Rd., Sturgeon Bay, WI 54235, Tel. 920/743 44 56, Fax 743 78 73*

HANNIBAL, MO

(114/A 5) A small harbour town like so many on the Mississippi River, with pretty alleyways off the residential streets and a picturesque Old Town. But Hannibal (Pop. 18,000) is famous for one of the greatest American writers who spent his youth here: Samuel Longhorn Clemens (1835–1910), better known as Mark Twain. He worked here as a river pilot, which is what gave him his name. "Mark Twain" means to mark two fathoms of water. He used his home town as a backdrop for the adventures of the famous figures in his novels, Tom Sawyer and Huckleberry Finn. No wonder the little town gets its living from literary tourism. Theatres produce Twain plays; a Mark Twain paddle steamer offers river tours, and you can even see the fence which Tom Sawyer had to paint in the novel.

MUSEUM

Mark Twain Boyhood Home
Mark Twain grew up in this little white house, and nearby a museum portrays his young days around 1850. *Open daily 8 am–6 pm in summer, other times 9 am–4*

pm, Sun midday–4 pm, admission US$ 6, 208 Hill Street

ACCOMMODATION

Garth Woodside Mansion
Eight rooms in a Victorian villa of 1871 which once belonged to a friend of Mark Twain. *RR3, Tel. 573/221 27 89, Category 2–3*

INDIANAPOLIS, IN

(115/D 5) A must for every motor racing enthusiast. Since 1911, on the last Sunday in May each year, the "Indy 500" has been run at the *Indianapolis Motor Speedway* in the north-west of the city; it is America's largest and most famous motor race and attracts more than 500,000 onlookers. Even when it is not actually a race day it is worth visiting the adjoining *Hall of Fame Museum* from which guided tours of the race track are offered daily.

Even if you are not keen on motor racing it is worth spending a day in the capital which, with a population of 1,500,000, is the largest city in Indiana – there are some good museums, and you can stroll through the historic quarter known as *Lockerbie Square* or enjoy a cappucino in a street café in the smart boutique district of *Broad Ripple* at the northern end of the city centre.

SURROUNDING AREA

Conner Prairie **(111/D 5)**
This large open air museum in the suburb of *Fishers* north-east of Indianapolis shows the life of the first settlers in Indiana. Exhibitions on the pioneering period, in

the summer concerts by the Indianapolis Symphony Orchestra. *Open only in summer Tue–Sat 9.30 am–5 pm, Sun 11 am–5 pm, admission US$ 9, 11601 Municipal Drive*

LAKE GENEVA, WI

(114/C 4) For more than a hundred years this lake and the town of the same name have been popular as a summer resort with city dwellers from Chicago which is only a two-hour drive away. Old villas are dotted along the wooded banks and there are good golf courses to attract the visitor. From Riviera Dock in the town the boats of the *Geneva Lake Cruise Line (Tel. 414/248 62 06)* provide excursions around the lake.

HOTEL

Grand Geneva Resort
Extensive holiday resort with spa, golf courses and tennis courts. *385 rooms, 7036 Grand Geneva Way, Tel. 414/248 88 11, Fax 249 47 63, category 1–2*

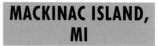

MACKINAC ISLAND, MI

(115/E 1) ★ Michilimackinac – "big turtle" was the name the Ojibwa Indians gave this rocky island (5 km long) which sits like a guard post at the narrow entrance to Lake Michigan. It was its strategic position which led the French, British and Americans to dispute possession in the 18th and 19th centuries of the island, and of *Mackinaw City*, the fortified town on the south bank.

At the end of the 19th century Mackinac Island became a holiday resort for the wealthy aristocracy of America – with Victorian villas with views over the pretty harbour where today ferries carrying day visitors from Mackinaw City berth. The Great Gatsby charms of the island are

The only traffic allowed on Mackinac Island are bicycles and horse-drawn coaches

jealously guarded, and all cars are banned – the only means of transport are bicycles and horse-drawn cabs. There is another attraction for car drivers: one of the world's longest suspension bridges (2543 m between the cable anchorings – twice as long as the Golden Gate Bridge) has spanned the strait since 1957. The little *Mackinac Bridge Museum (231 E. Central Av., Mackinaw City)* explains how this great project was built.

MUSEUMS

Colonial Michilimackinac

Wooden palisades, red-coated soldiers, missionaries and Indians – all is just as it was in the old British fort. *Open daily in summer 9 am–6 pm, admission US$ 7.25, Mackinaw City*

Fort Mackinac

◁▷ This massive 19th century stone fort tells of the varied military history of the Great Lakes. *Open daily in summer 9 am–6 pm, admission US$ 7.25, Mackinac Island*

INFORMATION

Mackinaw Tourist Bureau

708 S. Huron Av., Mackinaw City, MI 49 701, Tel. 616/436 56 64

MANITOWOC, WI

(114/C 3) The only ferry across Lake Michigan plies from here. In the high season you should reserve in advance for the four hour or so trip on the *S.S. Badger* to Ludington *Tel. 888/643 37 79, free of charge in the USA)*

MUSEUM

Wisconsin Maritime Museum

Located on the harbour, this museum documents the history of shipping on the lakes. *Open daily 9 am–6 pm, in winter Mon–Sat 9 am–5 pm, Sun 11 am–5 pm, admission US$ 4, 75 Maritime Drive*

HOTEL

Inn on Maritime Bay

◁▷ Beautifully situated on the harbour with a good restaurant and terrace. *107 rooms, 101 Maritime Dr., Tel. 920/682 70 00, Fax 682 70 13, Category 2–3*

MICHIGAN CITY, IN

(114/D 4) Gigantic industrial complexes stand on the south bank of Lake Michigan – including the five largest steel foundries in America – and yet here, scarcely an hour's drive from Chicago, there is also a holiday resort. Michigan City (Pop. 33,000) is popular with the people of Chicago as a convenient place for a day out. One reason is the opportunity to shop in the discount malls such as the *Lighthouse Place Outlet Center (6th/Wabash St.)*, but above all because of the *Indiana Dunes National Lakeshore*, a large recreation area and nature reserve. Along the banks of the lake there are nearly 30 km of bathing beaches and high dunes of quartz sand which was piled up by the waves after the Ice Age. In the *Dorothy Buell Visitor Center* on the corner of US12/Kemil Rd. you can obtain maps of walk trails in the dunes, moors and little forests in which rare plants and even cacti grow.

MILWAUKEE, WI

(114/C 3) A glance in the telephone book will quickly make it clear that this city (Pop. 1,800,000) in the state of Wisconsin has rightly been named the German city of America. As early as 1850 thousands of Germans emigrated to Wisconsin, a state with a very German feel. Most settled here on the west bank of Lake Michigan where there was a good natural harbour at the mouth of three rivers. *Millioki* – meeting place on the water – was the name the Indians had given this spot.

Towards the end of the 19th century the bulk of the population was of German origin. The town had six German daily newspapers at that time – and 25 breweries which gave Milwaukee a reputation as the stronghold of brewing in America. In addition, however, large tool factories and vehicle works such as Harley-Davidson soon sprang up, earning the town the further nickname of the "workbench of America".

Present-day Milwaukee has become truly American, German influence vanished with the First World War, and only one of the large breweries now remains. However, a Teutonic flair can still be detected in the many German restaurants and at the big festivals such as the *German Fest* at the end of July.

SIGHTS

City
The actual inner city lies somewhat further west on the Milwaukee River. In happy proximity around the main streets of *Wisconsin* and *Killbourn* *Avenue* can be found modern shopping complexes such as *Grand Avenue Mall* and Old Town streets like *Old World Third Street* with its German bakeries and butchers. You should also visit the restaurant and pub quarter around *Water Street* on the east side of the river.

Harley Davidson Inc.
A factory visit for motor cycle fans – all kinds of machines are made here. *Mon–Fri guided tours on request. 3700 W. Juneau Av., Tel. 414/343 46 80*

Juneau Park
⚓Large parks lie along the bank of Lake Michigan. Especially popular is Juneau Park with its idyllic lagoon and large marina. Around *Prospect Avenue* on the cliffs above stand some lovely old villas owned by rich brewery barons around 1900.

Turner Hall
⚡Typical of the German heyday is this historic brick building owned by the Milwaukee gymnastic club which was politically very active c. 1900. Guided tours on request. Restaurant inside. *1034 N. 4th St., Tel. 414/272 17 33*

MUSEUMS

Milwaukee Art Museum
This museum south of Juneau Park on the bank of the lake is worth a visit. On display is a wide spectrum of paintings ranging from works by German to Haitian artists. *Closed on Mon. Admission US$ 5, 750 N. Lincoln Memorial Drive*

Brew City BBQ
❧ Spare ribs with a fantastic sauce, with good beer and plenty going on in the nightlife quarter. *1114 N. Water St., Tel. 414/278 70 33, Category 2–3*

SHOPPING

House of Harley
Everything a Harley motorcyclist can desire – from a horn to a leather jacket. *6221 W. Layton Avenue*

HOTELS

Park East
A good middle class hotel on the eastern edge of the town centre. From the uppermost of the 159 rooms there is a fine view over the lake. *916 E. State St., Tel. 414/276 88 00, Fax 765 19 19, Category 2–3*

Pfister
A stylish grand hotel built in 1893: richly decorated lobby, cast iron balcony, elegant rooms with every comfort. *307 rooms, 424 E. Wiscinsin Av., Tel. 414/273 82 22, Fax 273 07 47, Category 1*

INFORMATION

Milwaukee Visitors Bureau
510 W. Kilbourn Av., Milwaukee, WI 53203, Tel. 414/273 72 22, Fax 273 55 96

SURROUNDING AREA

Cedarburg (114/C 3)
This pretty little historic township (Pop. 10,000), an hour's drive north of Milwaukee, is a popular point of departure for trips and cycle tours in the idyllic hilly countryside round about. This is the region of the *Kettle Moraine*, a long morainic chain from the Late Ice Age. A *scenic drive* – particularly beautiful in the glorious autumn colours – follows the hills northward past small lakes and through historic villages such as *Greenbush*.

OSHKOSH, WI

(114/C 3) This little township (Pop. 55,000) in the green heart of Wisconsin is known to mothers and fathers all over the world as the place where smart children's clothing is made. For those interested in aircraft Oshkosh has another attraction: the *EAA Air Adventure Museum (Open Mon–Sat 8.30 am–5 pm, Sun 11 am–5 pm, 3000 Poberezmy Rd., admission US$ 7.50)*, which displays nearly 100 experimental and some really bizarre aircraft. At the end of July each year thousands of pilots meet here with aircraft they have often made themselves in order to attend the "International Fly-in".

PETOSKEY, MI

(115/D 2) By the beginning of the 20th century this little harbour town on picturesque *Little Traverse Bay* was already a favourite with well-to-do summer holidaymakers. Impressive Victorian houses and pretty avenues in the suburb of *Bay View* testify to that. Also worth a visit is the little picture book town of *Harbor Springs* on the opposite side of the bay.

ACCOMMODATION

Terrace Inn
A nice B & B inn in a classic holiday hotel dating from 1909. *16 rooms,*

1549 Glendale St., Tel. 616/347 24 10, Fax 347 24 07, Category 2–3

ST LOUIS, MO

(114/B 6) Around 1850 this town at the confluence of the Missouri and Mississippi Rivers was the "Gateway to the West" for hundreds of thousands of pioneers. In the 20th century its breweries, motor car and aircraft factories made St Louis one of America's major industrial cities and today, with its population of over 2,500,000, it is the largest in the whole Mississippi Valley.

SIGHTS

City

During the 1980s St Louis made a start on revamping its sadly dilapidated inner city area around *Market Street.* As a result, the old warehouses in the historic *Laclede's Landing* quarter now house boutiques and restaurants, and *Union Station (1894)*, on the corner of Market and 18th St., once a springboard for settlers going west, has been superbly restored. At the western end of Downtown lies *Forest Park,* covering some 500 ha. As well as the excellent *St Louis Zoo* the sole building remaining from the 1904 World Exhibition has been made into the *St Louis Art Museum* (many works by German Impressionists).

Gateway Arch

⬳ This 192 m high steel arch on the Mississippi is the symbol of St Louis. It was built in 1965 as a memorial to the westward expansion by the American pioneers. There is a museum at its foot. *Open daily 8 am–10 pm, in winter 9 am–6 pm, admission US$ 2, elevator US$ 2.50, Riverfront Park*

HOTELS

Hyatt Regency Union Station

542 luxury rooms in the old station. *One St Louis Union Station, Tel. 314/231 12 34. Fax 923 39 70, Category 1–2*

The restored houses in the city of St Louis remind us of the pioneering period

Regal Riverfront
❖ A good middle class hotel on the river bank. There is a fine view from the revolving restaurant on the top floor. *780 rooms, 200 S. 4th St., Tel. 314/241 95 00, Fax 421 61 71, Category 2*

Studebaker National Museum
A dream come true for chrome fans: all Studebaker models from the 1920s until the firm closed down in 1966. *Open daily 9 am–5 pm, Sun from midday, admission US$ 4.50, 525 S. Main Street*

SURROUNDING AREA

Cahokia Mounds, Il   (114/B 6)
★ Around 65 large, pyramid-shaped *mounds* on the east bank of the Mississippi near Collinsville bear witness to North America's great prehistoric culture which flourished here between AD 700 and 1500, when some 20,000 Indians lived in Cahokia. The *mounds* – now designated a World Cultural Heritage site by UNESC0 – served as burial sites and platforms for temples. *Monks Mound*, the largest remaining mound, covers an area of almost six hectares and reaches a height of 30 m in four stages. There is a good exhibition centre portraying the way the Mississippi Indians lived. *Open daily 9 am–5 pm, admission free, Collinsville Road*

SOUTH BEND, IN

(115/D 4) Scarcely two hours' drive east of Chicago lies South Bend (Pop. 105,000), in the midst of fertile Indiana farmland. In the USA the town is known above all for its excellent *University of Notre Dame* with its extensive campus (*guided tours Mon–Fri*). The town is also home to an American legend: Studebaker cars. The Studebaker family originally built Conestoga wagons for trains taking pioneers going west, and then later it turned to making the legendary cult motor cars.

SURROUNDING AREA

Amish Country   (115/D 4)
★ East of South Bend lies the old-fashioned and devout world of Amish, Mennonite farmers with stern religious beliefs who reject all modern technology and live strictly pacifist lives. Like their forefathers, immigrants from Switzerland and Germany, they till the soil with horse-drawn ploughs and wear only sober black clothes. They are often seen driving their simple carts along the edge of the highways.

In the *Elkhardt (219 Caravan Dr., Tel. 219/262 81 61)* Visitors Center you can obtain a brochure showing the way to the main villages in Amish Country: to *Nappanee,* where you can visit a farm at least 100 years old in the *Amish Acres (Open daily 10 am–6 pm)* museum village, and to *Shipshewana (flea market on Tue, Wed, horse auction on Fri)*, where on Route 5 the culture centre of *Menno-Hof (Open Mon–Sat 10 am–5 pm)* documents in a very feeling way the religion and wanderings of the Amish people.

SPRINGFIELD, IL

(114/B 5) The capital of the state of Illinois has a population of only 100,000; it lies on the historic *Route 66* and is known mainly as the birthplace of Abraham Lincoln, who abolished slavery when he was President of the USA. You can visit his house in the *Lincoln Home National Historic Site (Open daily, admission free, 8th/Jackson St.)* and the mausoleum in which he is laid to rest in *Oak Ridge Cemetery*. The museum village of *Lincoln's New Salem (Open daily, admission free)* in the suburb of Petersburg illustrates with the help of log cabins the pioneer period during which he lived here. Also worth a visit is *Dana-Thomas House (closed Mon, Tue, admission free, 301 E. Lawrence St.)*, with original furniture and one of the best examples of the Prairie style adopted by famous architects.

SPRING GREEN, WI

(114/B 3) Hardly anybody would ever have heard of this tiny little farming town in the west of Wisconsin if it had not been for Frank Lloyd Wright who lived and worked here for almost 50 years.

As a result Spring Green became a place of pilgrimage for people from all over the world who were interested in architecture and wished to see Wright's private house and studio at first hand.

SIGHTS

House on the Rocks

★ This angular group of houses high up on a cliff is home to some immensely droll exhibits: historic circus organs and doll's houses, gigantic jukeboxes and knights' armour, Chinese jade work and the world's largest carousel. On balance, a fascinating piece of America. *Open in summer 10 am–8 pm, admission US$ 14.70, SR 23, 15 km south of Spring Green*

Taliesin

★ Scattered in a 250 ha park lie Wright's private house, studio and his school of architecture, all in buildings which

Where architects seek their master: the private house of the famous architect F.L. Wright

Route 66: Highway of Yearning

"Get your kicks on Route 66 ...", so sang the legendary Nat King Cole, getting to the very heart of the yearning for travel that was prevalent in the 1950s. He sang of the legendary *Mother Road*, the first road laid down in Western America in the 1920s, a 3,600 km-long road from Chicago to L.A. In the 1930s impoverished farmers from Oklahoma travelled westwards along Route 66 to the promised land of California, and in the 1950s the first tourists used it to visit the Grand Canyon. Some well-signposted nostalgic sections have been preserved at the start of the road in Illinois, parallel to the modern highway I–55. The finest sections are in Wilmington and Dwight in the north and also south of Springfield around Lichfield, Mount OLive and Staunton. And some old-fashioned reminders of Route 66 are still preserved: "Shea's", possibly the oldest filling station *(2075 Peoria Rd.)* and the classic diner "Cozy Drive-In" *(2935 S. 6th St.)* in Springfield.

the master himself designed between 1902 and 1953. *Guided tours daily, reservations recommended, Tel. 608/588 79 00, SR 23, 5 km south of Spring Green*

TRAVERSE CITY, MI

(115/D 2) Motley crowds on the long beaches, fast food outlets and motels are the main features in summer of this resort (Pop. 15,000) on the south shore of Grand Traverse Bay. You will find things are quieter and more idyllic outside the city as you drive or cycle along the ⬏panoramic roads along Lake Michigan. The SR 37 leads through cherry plantations and vineyards on the *Old Mission Peninsula* with an Indian mission church and an old lighthouse at the end. The SR 22 goes to the *Leelanau Peninsula*, also with an 1825 lighthouse which today houses a museum.

SURROUNDING AREA

Sleeping Bear Dunes   (115/D 2)
★ One of the most impressive natural wonders on the Great Lakes. There are more than 30 kilometres of massive dunes along the banks of Lake Michigan, built up by sand left behind by glaciers and blown here by the west wind. They get their name from an old Indian legend, which tells of a mother bear who fled with her young into the lake to escape from a forest fire. The young were drowned, and since then the grieving mother has lain waiting in the form of a giant dune on the banks of Lake Michigan. The dunes are up to 140 m high, and through them runs the 13 km-long ⬏*Pierce Stocking Scenic Drive* in the south of this nature reserve. A beautiful day excursion on water is the boat trip from the pretty fishing village of *Leland* to the *Manitou Islands*, two wilderness islands lying off the coast.

Through Chicago on foot

These walking tours are marked in green on the map on the back cover and in the Street Atlas beginning on page 106

① LOOK UP: SKYSCRAPERS IN AND AROUND THE LOOP

Johnny Head-in-the-Air goes through Chicago. On this tour you will constantly be looking upwards, at the tops of the legendary skyscrapers which were, so to speak, invented in Chicago and which tell of the city's architectural development (duration: approx. four hours).

From nostalgic skyscraper to futuristic glass box – this walk takes you through one hundred years of skyscraper architecture. World-famous architects like Frank Lloyd Wright, Ludwig Mies and Helmut Jahn have left their indelible stamp upon the city, from the end of the 19th century and into the new millenium. The starting point is the Michigan Avenue Bridge, an ideal rendezvous on the Chicago River. It leads south over Michigan Avenue to the *Carbide and Carbon Building (page 27)* which stands on a black plinth outside the Loop and is one of the city's finest buildings. The green terracotta cladding has lost much of its sparkle but at the top the dainty gold leaf ornamentation still gleams. Our walk continues by way of Lake Street and along the eastern edge of the Loop. Michigan Avenue, swept clean by the squalls which blow through the "Windy City", lies majestically between Grant Park and the Loop. To the right the legendary El rattles along on its high rails. Between Randolph and Washington Street lies the *Chicago Cultural Center*, an exhibition and concert centre, built in 1897, the Grandezza of which is reminiscent of palaces in Florence and Venice.

Now follow Madison Street westwards, go under the noisy El and into the Loop, the city's busy centre. Continue south via State Street, the city's legendary business street. The attempt to convert this former traffic artery into a pedestrian zone was fundamentally flawed and cars have been running along State Street for some years now. However, this adds to the large city feeling. It is nearly always the rush hour in Chicago. Between Madison and Monroe Street the skyscraper of the *Carson Pirie Scott and Company Store* is one of the most courageous buildings by the unconventional architect Louis H. Sullivan, who emphasised the height of the edifice by the use of dynamic ornamentation and slender columns inside. Then turn right into Van Buren Street, go past the Harold Washington Library, the grim façade of which is redolent of a giant mausoleum, to the *Monadnock Building (page 28)*, which lies on Dearborn Street between Van Buren and Jackson. It is a fine example of the Chicago School of Architecture and when it was built was the largest office building anywhere in the world. It was the credo of the architects of the time that all shapes and ornamentation should emphasise the function of a building, and that is demonstrated to perfection in this sober brick edifice of 1891. Proceed via Jackson Street to LaSalle Street and to the *Chicago Board of Trade (page 27)*, the most beautiful skyscraper of the art deco era with a statue of Ceres, the goddess of agriculture, on the top. The cuboid black *Sears Tower (page 15)* towers up into the sky on Wacker Drive; until a few years ago it was the tallest building in the world and there is a superb view from the top. If you wish you can now savour a few delicacies at Mrs Levy's *(page 49)*.

Our walk then leads back east via Adams Street. Just before Clark Street visit *Rookery Building (page 29)*, with its magnifi-cently impressive marble foyer. Frank Lloyd Wright designed it in the early 1920s. Follow Clark Street northwards and then take a rest in the sun on the First National Plaza (if the weather is favourable). There are plenty of chairs available. Here you can enjoy a hot dog, just like most of the workers taking their lunch break here. Before continuing east along Randolph Street visit the futuristic *James R. Thompson Center (page 28)* by the German architect Helmut Jahn, the glass and steel construction of which is redolent of a spaceship. Continue left into State Street, then right into Lake Street and by way of Wabash and South Street back to Michigan Avenue. On the far side of the bridge the 1924 *Wrigley Building (page 13)* is one of the city's best known skyscrapers. Opposite it the *Chicago Tribune Tower (pages 27–28)* marks the end of this long walk. Enough of architecture. Now plunge into the shoppers' paradise, Michigan Avenue, dominated by the black tower of the *John Hancock Center (page 14)*.

② HOUSES BELONGING TO THE TOP TEN THOUSAND: THE GOLD COAST TOUR

The Gold Coast earned its name in the period after the Great Fire (1871), when well-heeled citizens built magnificent villas on North Astor Street in particular. Goethe Street and Schiller Street are reminders of the German immigrants who settled here. Duration of the walk: approx. three hours.

The walk begins at Oak Street Beach, the popular beach between Lake Shore Drive and

Lake Michigan. Even during the week the asphalted paths are used by cyclists and skateboarders, and on sunny days the sand becomes a play area for sun-hungry urban visitors. The beach is part of the Gold Coast, which owes its name to the wealthy citizens who built villas here after the Great Fire of 1871. Large numbers of German immigrants also settled in this part of the city. Going through the underpass brings you to Division Street, then turn right into North Astor Street on which lie most of the splendid houses owned by the "top ten thousand". At the junction of Astor and Goethe Street are several prime addresses: *1316* and *1322 North Astor* were built c. 1930 by Philip B. Maher, and are two outstanding examples of the modern, functional design adopted after the First World War. The *James L. Houghteling Houses (1308* and *1312 N. Astor)* were completed in 1888 and are two of the finest town houses of the period.

From Goethe to Schiller: at the junction of Astor/Schiller Street and to the north thereof lie *Charnley-Persky House (1365 N. Astor)*, designed by Frank Lloyd Wright and other architects and regarded as the first modern house in America, *Joseph T. Ryerson House (1406 N. Astor)*, built in 1922, *1444 N. Astor*, redolent of the art deco skyscrapers in the city centre, and *Tudor House (1451 N. Astor)*, with its narrow windows. At East Burton Place proceed left past the *Patteson-McCormack Mansion (20 E. Burton)*, an Italian palazzo which

could easily be in Venice and was a birthday present to his daughter from the publisher of the Chicago Tribune.

Our tour continues via North Street to North Boulevard, where the seat of the Roman Catholic archbishop, a red brick-built house, is reminiscent of "olde England". The *Chicago Historical Society*, housed in a large building by Lincoln Park, is worth a visit, although you should allow an extra hour for this if you are interested in the city's history. Relaxation is the order of the day in North Wells Street, a turning two blocks further south. It leads through the *Old Town (page 25)*, one of the city's entertainment districts, and has some enticing restaurants, street cafés and shops. Return to the beach by way of East Goethe, North Astor and East Division Street.

③ ART IN THE OPEN AIR: THE LOOP SCULPTURE TOUR

Sculptures are scattered about in the Loop as in an open-air museum. A walk through this "open-air museum" does not cost a cent and takes you through the busy centre of the Windy City (duration: two hours).

This tour starts in the Loop at the corner of Dearborn and Jackson Street, at the Red and Blue Lines of the Jackson subway station, in the midst of the hustle and bustle on the city's busiest streets. Not quite the normal backcloth for an art museum. But why should art not be displayed where as many people as possible can see it?

This was made possible in the city of Chicago. Anyone disembarking in the subway will see four sculptures: "The Town-Ho"s Story", by Frank Stella, "Ruins III", by Nita K. Sutherland, "Lines in Four Directions" by Sol Lewitt and one of the finest sculptures in the Loop, the orange-coloured "Flamingo" by Alexander Calder in front of the Federal Center; it is an elegant steel construction with bold wings which reminded the artist of a flamingo. Nobody minds that children play beneath the sculpture.

Clark Street takes you south and Van Buren Street west. Between LaSalle and Sherman Street stands "San Marco II", fashioned in 1986 by Ludovico de Luigi. Then follow Wacker Drive to the right as far as Adams Street. The "Gem of the Lakes" was the work of Raymond Kaskey in 1990. In the foyer of *Sears Tower (page 15)* stands a second sculpture by Alexander Calder, "The Universe". Now proceed east via Adams Street and north via Wells Street. Between Monroe and Madison Street are works by Frank Stella, "Loomings" and "Knights and Squires", while between Madison and Washington Street stands "Down Shadows" by Louise Nevelson. The sculptures seem to rise naturally out of the stone desert and are like oases of colour among the skyscrapers and glass palaces.

Proceed eastwards by way of Randolph Street. At North LaSalle Street towers the imaginative sculpture "Freeform" by Richard Hunt, and "Flight of Daedalus and Icarus" symbolises the first attempt by man to fly. This sculpture is by Roger Brown. "The Monument with Standing Beasts", a work by Jean Dubuffet which was unveiled on his 84th birthday in 1985, tries to compete with the striking *James R. Thompson Center (page 28)* by Helmut Jahn with its colour scheme of red, orange and silver. A lot of court sittings are held in the Daley Center, but the visitor will enjoy more fully the statue by Pablo Picasso. This 160 tonne work has stood on this spot since 1967; it is an abstract being, part woman, part butterfly, part beast of prey, more tolerated than liked by the people of Chicago. From Dearborn enter Washington Street, to "Miro's Chicago", an abstract female with outstretched arms which was unveiled in 1981 on Miro's 88th birthday. The final work in this "museum without walls" is the 13 m wide mosaic "The Four Seasons", which Marc Chagall sculpted in 1975 and presented to one of his favourite cities. This tour through the Loop ends here in front of the busy First National Plaza.

Practical information

This section lists all the essential addresses and information you need for your holiday in Chicago

AMERICAN & BRITISH ENGLISH

Marco Polo travel guides are written in British English. In North America certain terms and usages deviate from British usage. Some of the more frequently encountered examples are (American given first): *baggage = luggage; cab = taxi; car rental = car hire; drugstore = chemist; fall = autumn; first floor = ground floor; freeway/highway = motorway; gas(oline) = petrol; railroad = railway; restroom = toilet/lavatory; streetcar = tram; subway = underground/tube; toll-free numbers = freephone numbers; trailer = caravan; trunk = boot (of a car); vacation = holiday; wait staff = waiter/waitress; zip code = post code.*

CUSTOMS

Entry into the USA: you are allowed to bring in one US gallon (3.61 litres) of alcohol, 200 cigarettes or 100 cigarillos or 50 cigars or 50 g of tobacco and gifts valued at up to US$ 100. Unwrapped food, fruit and vegetables can be retained. Entry to the UK: 1 litre of alcohol (over 22 per cent proof), or 2 litres of wine, 200 cigarettes or 100 cigarillos or 50 cigars or 250 g of tobacco, 50 ml of perfume and gifts valued at up to £100.

EMBASSIES & CONSULATES

British Consulate-General

13th Floor, The Wrigley Building
400 N Michigan Avenue
Chicago IL 60611
Tel. 312/346 18 10, Fax: 312/464 06 61

Canadian Consulate General
Two Prudential Plaza
180 North Stetson Avenue, Suite 2400
Chicago IL 60601
Tel. 312/616 18 60, Fax: 312/616 18 77

EMERGENCIES

In the event of accidents or emergencies telephone *911*. This connects you to the police, fire brigade or ambulance.

HEALTH

The standard of medical care in the United States is high, both as regards the numbers and competence of doctors and dentists and in the hospitals. The only problem for visitors is likely to be the high cost: a stay in hospital in particular is extremely expensive. It is essential, therefore, to make sure, before leaving home, that you have adequate insurance cover.

The supply of medicines is also well organised. Visitors who regularly need a particular medicine should take a copy of the prescription with them so that it can be re-issued by an American doctor if necessary.

The recommended hospital in Chicago is the *Northwestern Memorial Hospital, Streeterville, Tel. 312/908 20 00*

PRE-TRAVEL INFORMATION

The US does not maintain a network of national tourist offices abroad, nor do US embassies or consulates provide a tourist information service. Information about Chicago is available from the Illinois Bureau of Tourism's web site at *http://www.enjoyillinois.com*

INFORMATION IN CHICAGO

Chicago Office of Tourism
Chicago Cultural Center, 78 E. Washington St., Chicago, IL 60602, Tel. 312/744 24 00, Fax 744 23 59
Visitor Center
77 E. Randolph St., Chicago, Mon–Fri 10 am–6 pm, Sat 10 am–5 pm, Sun midday–5 pm
Historic Water Tower Visitor Welcome Center
Chicago Av., and Michigan Av., summer: Mon–Fri 9.30 am–7 pm, Sat 10 am–6 pm, Sun 11 am–5 pm, winter: Mon–Fri 9.30 am–6 pm, Sat 10 am–6 pm, Sun 11 am–5 pm
Illinois Market Place Visitor Information Center
Navy Pier, 700 E. Grand Av., Chicago, Mon–Thu 10 am–8 pm, Fri, Sat 10 am–11 pm, Sun 10 am–7 pm

LOST AND FOUND

Traveler's Aid will assist in tracing lost luggae: *Tel. 773/894 24 27.* Please telephone the police in all cases of theft or loss.

MONEY

The unit of currency in the USA is the dollar. One dollar equals 100 cents. There are one cent *(penny),* five cents *(nickel),* ten cents *(dime),* 25 cents *(quarter)* and, more rarely, 50 cents and one dollar coins. Banknotes are in denominations of one, two, five, ten, 20, 50 and 100 dollars. All notes are the same size and colour and thus difficult to differentiate.

The exchange rate is more favourable in Europe, so obtain your currency before leaving home if possible, with part in US dollar traveller's cheques which are accepted almost everywhere just like cash. Eurocheques are not accepted. Strongly recommended (almost essential in hotels or when renting a car) is a credit card, if possible Mastercard or Visa, these being the most common in the USA.

Bank opening times: Mon–Fri 9 am–3 or 4 pm. Bureaux de change in Chicago: Rush St. Currency Exchange, 12 E. Walton St., Tel. 312/71 17; World's Money Exchange, 6 E. Randolph St., Suite 204, Tel. 312/641 21 51

NEWSPAPERS

The *Chicago Tribune* is a quality newspaper, the *Chicago Sun-Times* is one of the better tabloids. The best information is contained in the nation-wide tabloid *USA Today.* British papers can be found at the airport and in special shops. Information about current events in the Chicago area is provided in the two free publications *Chicago Official Visitor Guide* and *Key This Week,* obtainable in the tourist information centres.

PASSPORTS & VISAS

A passport (valid for at least a further six months) is sufficient for a stay of up to 90 days. A visitor's visa is no longer necessary. It is sufficient to complete a *Pilot Waiver Program*, which is distributed at the airport.

POST

Post office opening times: *Mon–Fri 8 am–6 pm, Sat 8 am–midday; head post office: 433 W. Harrison St., south of the Loop*

PUBLIC TRANSPORT

Unlike most other American cities, Chicago has a first-class public transport system. The buses and railways (the El elevated railway and the underground/subway) run by the *Chicago Transit Authority (CTA)* form a dense network. A single journey costs US$ 1.50, plus 30 cents for a transfer. Chargeable magnetic cards are available from slot machines. The cheapest way for visitors to travel is with budget one, two or three visitor passes obtainable from selected stations and from Visitors Service Centers.

SALES TAX

In Chicago a sales tax of 8.75 per cent is added to prices. In inner city restaurants it is 9.75 per cent. The room tax in hotels is a princely 14.9 per cent.

TAXIS

Taxis cost less than in many European cities but do not all have the same type of number plate. Some

firms: *Yellow Cab, Tel. 312/TAXI-CAB; Flash Cab, Tel. 773/561 14 44, Checker Cab, Tel. 312/CHECKER*

TICKETS

Tickets for most performances and events can be ordered by telephone using your credit card from: *Ticketmaster, Tel. 312/559 12 12, www.ticketmaster.com* or *Ticket Exchange, Tel. 1800-666-07 79*. On the day of the event tickets are half price from *Hot Tix Ticket Centers, Tel. 312/977 17 55*. They have to be collected in person from one of their numerous outlets, e.g. *108 N. State St., Historic Water Tower Visitor Information Center, Bloomingdales.*

TIPPING

There is little in Chicago that does not involve a tip: in restaurants and taxis it is customary to give 15–20 per cent of the bill, a porter expects a dollar per suitcase, and for room service it is usual to tip one dollar per night. Every service should be rewarded with a tip.

TOURS

City tours to places of interest in the city centre and suburbs of Chicago: *Gray Line of Chicago* (several tours): *Tel. 312/251 31 07; Chicago Trolley Company* (rubber-tyred cable cars run through the city centre and stop every 20 minutes in front of attractions such as Navy Pier and Sears Tower): *Tel. 312/663 02 60.* Tours to places of architectural interest (by boat, bus or on foot): *Chicago Architecture Foundation, 224 S. Michigan Av., Tel. 312/922 34 32.* By boat across Lake Michigan: *The Spirit of Chicago* (round tours, dinner cruises with cabaret, approx. US$

25–75), *Navy Pier, tel. 312/836 78
99.* In the footsteps of Al Capone
and co.: *Untouchable Tours, Tel.
773/881 11 95*

VOLTAGE

Electricity in the USA is 110
volts AC. Electrical appliances
must therefore be adjustable to
that voltage and adaptors (obtainable in most stores) will be
required since American sockets
are different from British and
other European ones.

WEIGHTS & MEASURES

1 cm	0.39 inch
1 m	1.09 yd (3.28 ft)
1 km	0.62 miles
1 sq m	1.20 sq yds
1 ha	2.47 acres
1 sq km	0.39 sq miles
1 g	0.035 ounces
1 kg	2.21 pounds
1 British ton	1016 kg
1 US ton	907 kg

*1 litre is equivalent to 0.22 Imperial
gallons and 0.26 US gallons*

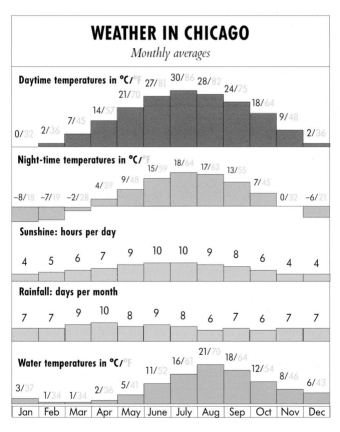

Do's and don'ts

You can experience some nasty surprises in Chicago too.
Tourist traps, faux pas – and how to avoid them

Topless bathing

Oak Street Beach at the northern end of the Magnificent Mile and North Avenue Beach six blocks further north are among the most popular beaches on Lake Michigan. But even though Chicago is an enlightened city women should never bathe topless. At the very least attract curious and disapproving looks or even a reprimand from the law.

Lack of respect towards the police

American policemen have little sense of humour and act with far less consideration than their European colleagues when they are on the trail of a suspect. Americans know that and stay in their car with their hands on the steering wheel when they are stopped, even though they may have done nothing wrong. You should do exactly the same and show the necessary respect for the law. On the other hand, the cops are friendly if you ask them the way and they will even help if you break down.

Smoking

The USA is becoming a country of non-smokers. Smoking is prohibited in all public buildings, many restaurants, even in some hired cars. Things are not as strict in Chicago as they are in California, but smokers should nevertheless refrain from lighting up and ask politely if there is a "smoking zone".

Going through West Side with a bulging wallet

The crime rate in Chicago is higher than in most European cities, but that is no reason to panic. If you take the necessary care, do not display an expensive Rolex on your wrist or flash one hundred dollar bills about you have little to fear. As in London or Paris, however, when in Chicago at night you should avoid dark corners, deserted railway stations or empty streets. Take a taxi! And for goodness' sake do not drive in the West Side – gang wars still rage there, at least in some streets.

Street Atlas of Chicago

Please refer to back cover for an overview of this Street Atlas

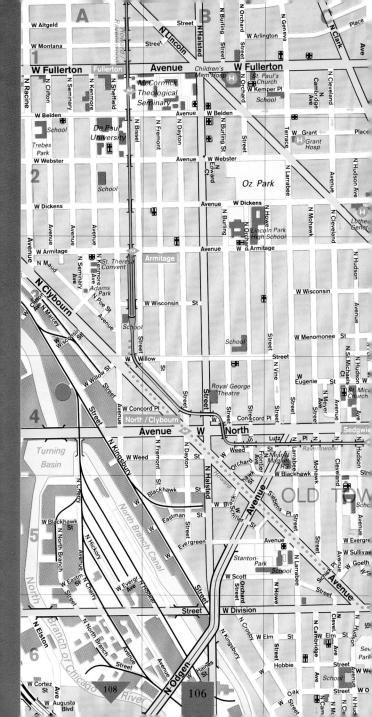

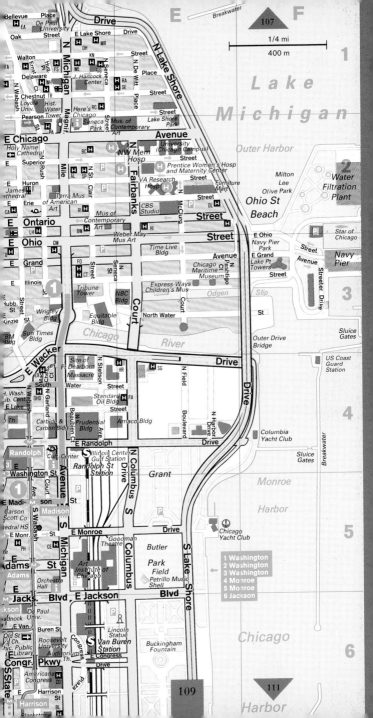

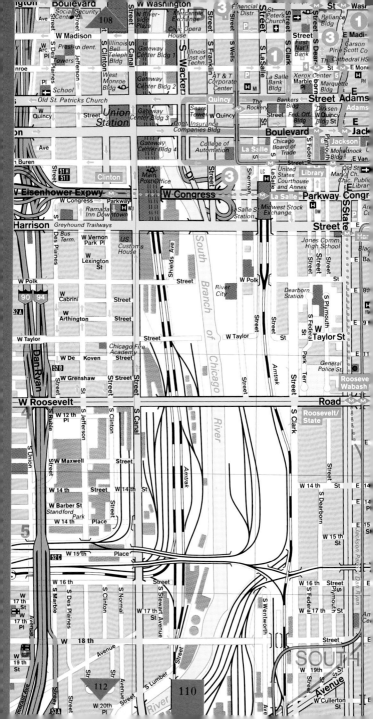

Station

Grant

Monroe

109

1/4 mi

400 m

1

Columbus

E Monroe

Drive

Chicago
Yacht Club

adison

St

Goodman
Theatre

Butler

Park

Field

1 Washington
2 Washington
3 Washington
4 Monroe
5 Monroe
6 Jackson

St

Michigan

Petrillo Music
Shelf

Art
Institute
of Chicago

Blvd

E Jackson

Columbus

S Lake Shore

Blvd

Lincoln
Statue

Chicago

2

osevelt
versity
Auditorium
Th.

S Van Buren
Station

E Congress

Buckingham
Fountain

Congress
Plaza

Drive

rrison
St

BL

CH

41

a
Spertus Museum
Ave of E Balbo
Judaica

Harbor

Drive

treet

AS

Tennis
Courts

3

Grant

Hutchinson

Field

ast-West-
niversity
treet

L a k e

Street

AS

AV

Drive

Park

M i c h i g a n

osevelt

Rd

Roosevelt
Dr

Columbus
Mem

John G. Shedd
Aquarium

Breakwater

Adler
Planetarium

4

S Roosevelt
Rd Station

S Lake Shore

E Solidarity

Drive

Northerly Island
Park

13th

St

S Indiana

Pasteur
Mon

Field Museum
of Natural History

Bath House
12th St
Beach

Circuit Court of
Cook County

McFetridge

Drive

Burnham Pt
Yacht Club

Linn

chool

Street

H

Chicago Park
District
Administ.
Bldg.

Burnham

White

5

Avenue

Metra

Soldier
Field

16th

Street

S Indiana

S Prairie

E
Wald ron

Drive

Park

Merrill C.

Meigs

an Police
and Museum

18th

Street

18th St
Station

18 th

S Calumet

Drive

Harbor

Field

6

OOP

Glessner House

Prairie Avenue
Historic District

Second
Presbyterian
Church

Clarke House

Cullerton

Street

111

Mc Cormick

113

Place

Chicago Technical

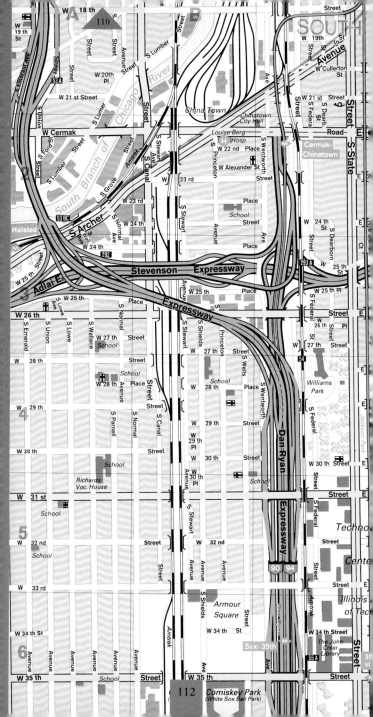

A 18th
110
W A 18th
B Street
W 19th St
W 19th St
Avenue
W Cullerton St
S Lumber
Street
Street
Street
S Emerald Ave
53 A
W 20th Pl
Chicago River
W 21st Street
W 21st Street
S Dearborn
S Federal
China Town
Chinatown City Hall
Louise-Berg
Hosp
Cermak-Chinatown
W Cermak
Road
State
S Ford St
S Lumber
Street
Street
Street
Amtrak
S Canal
Street
S Wentworth
Princeton
W 22nd Place
W Alexander St
Street
Cermak-Chinatown
S Union
S Lumber
South Branch of Chicago River
W 23rd
W
23rd
Place
Ave
S State
E
53 BC
S Grove
S Archer
S Wall
Ave
W 24th
Avenue
School
Street
W 24th St
S Dearborn
Halsted
S Archer
W 24th
Place
W 24th
Ave
S Stewart
Place
S Wentworth
Ave
Ct
292
293 A
W 25th St
Adlai E.
Stevenson Expressway
W 25th
Place
W 25th Pl
W 25th
Place
S Federal
Expressway
S Lowe
Ave
S Shields
Princeton
S
W 26th
Street
E
W 26th
S Emerald
S Union
S Lowe
S Wallace
W 27th
School
Street
S Stewart
S Wells
27th Street
Street
W 27th Street
54
Street
Street
School
S Wentworth
School
W 28th
Place
28th Place
Williams Park
S Federal
S Parnell
S Normal
W 28th
Avenue
W 29th
Street
Jackson Park
W 29th
S Canal
Street
Street
W 29th Pl
W 30th
Street
W 30th
Street
School
Richards Voc. House
Avenue
W 30th Pl
Dan-Ryan
School
W 31st
Street
E
School
Street
S Federal
Techno
W 32nd
School
Street
32nd
Avenue
Avenue
Street
Expressway
Cente
90 94
W 33rd
Street
Street
Illinois of Tec
Amtrak
W 34th St
Armour Square
S Shields
Street
W 34th St
W 34th Street
The John Crear Library
Avenue
Avenue
Avenue
Avenue
Avenue
55 A
Sox-35th
Street
W 35th
School
Street
W 35th
Ave
W 35th
Street
112
Comiskey Park
(White Sox Ball Park)

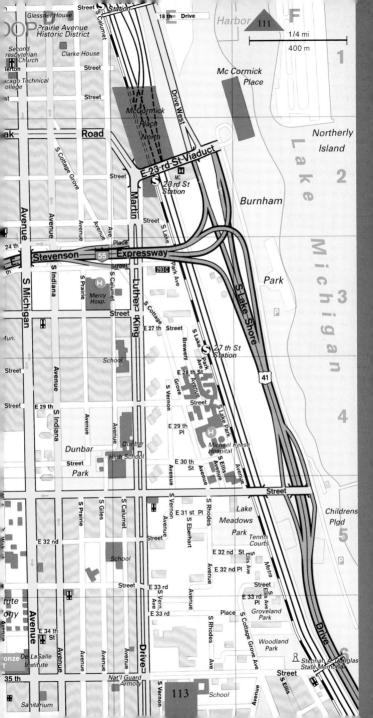

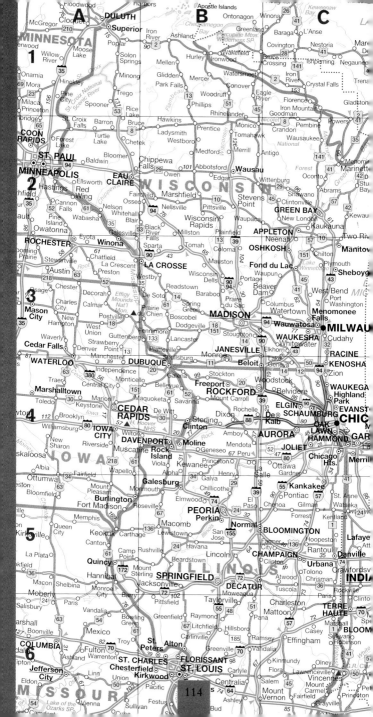

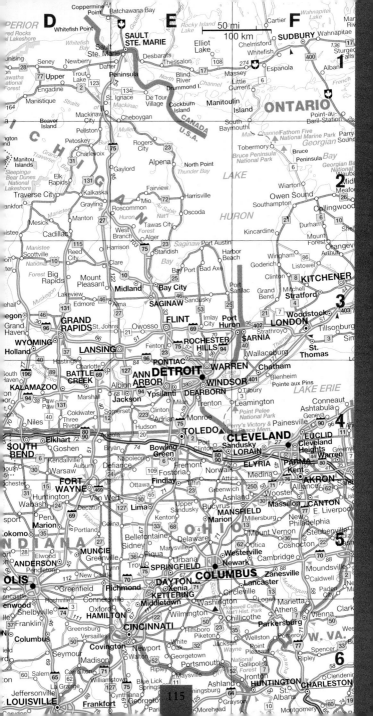

STREET ATLAS LEGEND

Freeway - Number of Junction Autobahn - Anschlußstellennummer	**56 A**	Autoroute - Numero d' échangeur Autosnelweg - Nummer van op- en afritten
Divided Highway Vierspurige Straße		Route à quatre voies Weg met vier rijstroken
Through Fare Durchgangsstraße		Route de transit Weg voor doorgaande verkeer
Main Road Hauptstraße		Route principale Hoofdweg
Other Roads Sonstige Straßen		Autres routes Overige wegen
Railway Bahnlinie		Chemin de fer Spoorweg
Subway U-Bahn	Ⓜ	Métro Ondergrondse spoorweg
Landing Place Anlegestelle	⚓	Embarcadère Aanlegplaats
Parking - One Way Street Parkplatz - Einbahnstraße	P →	Parking - Rue à sens unique Parkeerplaats - Straat met éénrichtingsverkeer
Church - Church of interest - Chapel Kirche - Sehenswerte Kirche - Kapelle	✠ ✠ ⊞	Église - Eglise remarquable - Chapelle Kerk - Bezienswaardige kerk - Kapel
Police Station - Post Office Polizeistation - Postamt	● ✉	Poste de police - Bureau de poste Politiebureau - Postkantoor
Monument Denkmal	𐐕	Monument Monument
Radio- or TV Tower - Lighthouse Funkturm - Leuchtturm	⚡ ⧖	Tour radio ou télévision - Phare Radio- of televisietoren - Vuurtoren
Hospital - Hotel Krankenhaus - Hotel	Ⓗ H	Hôpital - Hôtel Ziekenhuis - Hotel
Built-up Area - Public Building Bebauung - Öffentliches Gebäude		Zone bâtie - Bâtiment public Woongebied - Openbaar gebouw
Industrial Area Industriegebiet		Zone industrielle Industriekomplex
Park, Forest Park, Wald		Parc, bois Park, bos
Beach Strand		Plage Strand met zwemgelegenheid

Marco Polo Walking Tours

① Look up: skyscrapers in and around the Loop

② Houses belonging to the top ten thousand: the Gold Coast Tour

③ Art in the open air: the Loop Sculpture Tour

This index lists a selection of the streets and squares shown in the Street Atlas.

INDEX

This index lists all the main sights, museums, parks, and important buildings, restaurants and places around the Great Lakes, mentioned in this guide. Numbers in bold indicate a main entry, italics a photograph.

What do you get for your money?

You do not get anything for nothing in Chicago. You have to bear in mind that, generally speaking, the purchasing power of the dollar is about 65 British pence. However, in comparison with New York or San Francisco (or perhaps even London) the Windy City comes off quite well. A journey by El, subway or bus (to anywhere you wish within the city) costs US$ 1.50, a visitor pass entitling you to unlimited city travel on any one day is only US$ 5. For a taxi ride within the Loop you will have to pay less than US$ 5. A decent hotel room can cost between US$ 100 and 400. A Big Mac costs half as much as in Europe, while you can get a meal in a budget chain restaurant for about US$ 8. A Coke costs about US$ 1.50, coffee US$ 1. The price of a cinema ticket is US$ 8, theatre tickets range between US$ 10 and 80. And if you must rent a car petrol will cost you about one half of the European price.

You can pay by credit card in most restaurants, hotels and almost all shops. Travellers cheques are accepted almost everywhere, but Eurocheques are unknown.

£	US $	Can $	US $
1	1.49	1	0.67
2	2.98	2	1.34
3	4.47	3	2.01
4	5.96	4	2.68
5	7.45	5	3.35
10	14.90	10	6.70
15	22.35	15	10.05
20	29.80	20	13.40
25	37.25	25	16.75
30	44.70	30	20.10
40	59.60	40	26.80
50	74.50	50	33.50
60	89.40	60	40.20
70	104.30	70	46.90
80	119.20	80	53.60
90	134.10	90	60.30
100	149.00	100	67.00
200	298.00	200	134.00
300	447.00	300	201.00
400	596.00	400	268.00
500	745.00	500	335.00
750	1117.50	750	502.50
1,000	1490.00	1,000	670.00

These exchange rates are for guidance only and are correct at June 2000. You are advised to check with a bank or tourist office before travelling.